# Tradecraft

## For the Church on Mission

Urban Loft Publishers :: Portland, OR

Urban Loft Publishers
2034 NE 40th Avenue #414
Portland, OR 97212
www.theurbanloft.org

ISBN: 978-1479300914

Printed in the United States of America

Illustrations by Betsy Lance
www.BetsyLance.com                          Betsy.Lance@gmail.com

# Author Profiles

**Larry E McCrary** co-founded The Upstream Collective. He has a wonderful wife who loves working with Third-Culture Kids. His children Megan and Parker have spent most of their lives in Europe. They were involved in church planting in the States during the 90s and have been in Spain and Germany since 2001. He loves working with young churches and helping them begin to engage their community and their world.

**Caleb Crider** co-founded the Upstream Collective in Spain in 2007. He lives in Portland, Oregon, with his wife, two children, a dog, and some chickens. He works as a communications specialist, but he is really a missionary and church planter who believes that all Christians everywhere should think and act like missionaries.

**Wade Stephens** has lived on mission with his family for 10 years in Eastern Europe. For the past several years, he has been in the U.S. while helping churches, companies, and individuals that are seeking to live as missionaries. Working as a missionary and/or tentmaker over the years, he recognizes an opportunity for the gospel to advance through creative endeavors.

**Rodney Calfee** was a product of the Upstream Collective before he ever considered joining the team. He joined UC as a young pastor on a trip to Taiwan, where everything he knew about church planting and missional living was stretched and challenged. He works full-time with Upstream in Birmingham, where he lives with his wife and three daughters. His hope is that other leaders would have a similar experience to his and be impassioned and equipped to lead their people to think and act like missionaries.

# Endorsements

In this book the authors lovingly articulate the key missionary tactics and approaches that can unlock neighborhoods and cities for the Gospel. They have a long experience in these matters and are very well-read. Highly recommended as a handbook to missions anywhere.

**Alan Hirsch,**
Founder of Forge Mission Training Network and author of numerous award-winning books on missional Christianity.
www.theforgottenways.org

With *Tradecraft*, the leaders at Upstream are providing practical steps toward actual missional engagement. The nine missionary skills outlined in the book will help Christians live in mission-shaped ways, and engage their neighbors and the nations for the cause of Christ.

**Ed Stetzer,**
Missiologist, Church Planter/Pastor of Grace Church, and author of numerous books, including *Subversive Kingdom.* www.edstetzer.com

I've long thought that the principles we use to engage the nations with the gospel should be taught to a wider audience. That is exactly what *Tradecraft* has done. The guys at the Upstream Collective have written an outstanding book that I will use to train both our future missionaries and disciple believers in my local context. This is a book church leaders should read and get into the hands of their people.

**Nathan Garth,**
Global Pastor of Sojourn Community Church, Louisville, KY
www.international.sojournchurch.com

Much has been written recently about the mission of the church. Many churches are talking about "being missional" and "engaging their city." But while more people are grasping their role in God's mission, many still lack the tools to fulfill it. This book aims to fill some of that gap. In its nine chapters the authors, all experienced international missionaries, offer basic skills from international missions that they believe are foundational to the church no matter where you are. I don't think I've read a book that so clearly lays out these core missionary strategies. These are skills that the Western church needs. I would recommend *Tradecraft* for any pastor or leader who wants to understand how to better understand and engage their context. In particular, I think it could be a valuable tool for church planters or revitalizers who are trying to learn their context for the first time.

**J.D. Greear,**
Pastor of the Summit Church and author of several books, including *GOSPEL: Recovering the Power that Made Christianity Revolutionary.*
www.jdgreear.com

The church is facing a crisis in the US. Culture is shifting, and our methods for reaching the lost with the gospel have not. What do we do? We must learn to be missionaries right here at home. The guys at Upstream have given us a great gift in a book that will help us accomplish that goal. *Tradecraft* is an absolute must-have resource for those willing to answer His call. There is no published work like it.

**David Putman,**
Founder of the Planting the Gospel network and author of several books, including *Detox for the Overly Religious.*
www.plantingthegospel.com

# TABLE OF CONTENTS

# FOREWORD

BY JASON DUKES

*Embodiment.* It mattered enough to God that this became both the centerpiece and the climax of His communication with us. His has always been a message of love, and there can be no message of love without near presence. Thus, the Word became flesh and took up residence among us (John 1:14).

"Embodiment" is not a word that most people in American church culture ever utter. "Missionary" is, though. But do they really know what that means?

Theoretically, a "missionary" has been thought of as someone who might go to a people who are foreign, whether geographically or culturally, and communicate the gospel to them. Those missionaries who have seen some sort of transformational effect take place have done this communication of God's love – translation might be a better word – in two ways: among the people, and in the language and cultural nuances of the people.

Practically, a "missionary" has been supported and prayed for and encouraged and allowed to come back home and visit. They return to share stories, invoke emotions, and ask for more support. Checks are written. Every now and then, some emboldened, inspired soul asserts that some of us other folks should go on mission. A sign-up sheet appears in the hallway on the "missions" bulletin board. Some people visit the mission field. Missions acts are performed. They return home, usually praying more fervently for the host missionary, and very often yearning for something more. But when they meditate on what more could be done, going back "over there" is most commonly the conclusion.

But is this what Jesus intended?

Jesus did not do "missions" in this way. He did not come as a "missionary" in this way. His name "Emmanuel" sums up His missionary heart better than any other word – "God with us." And when was Jesus with the people? Everyday. And what did He do when He was with them? Eat. Drink. Serve. Converse. The rhythms of daily life.

Are we "missionaries" in that way too?

Jesus prayed in the garden the night before He gave up His life, "In the same way that You gave Me a mission in the world, I give them a mission in the world" (John 17:18, *The Message*).

This calling, along with much else of what Jesus taught, implies a life purpose for us as His followers that goes far beyond writing a check or taking a short trip.

The leaders of the Upstream Collective have posed the same question to many hopeful missionaries as I have: *How will we think and live like missionaries in the everyday rhythms of our lives wherever we are?*

This is not a question to be handled quickly and tritely. We must consider it, wrestle with it, give it time and space to come alive. Jesus prayed as such, that we should embrace the mission the Father intends for us. Something tells me that the product of our wrestling with such a question might lead to cultivation to occur "on earth as it is in heaven" wherever we go. Everyday. Everywhere. Something tells me thinking and acting like a "missionary" is not one of many ministry functions for followers of Jesus. It is THE function. Together. For every follower. In every context.

*Tradecraft* gets to the heart of how to embody this thinking and living like a missionary unlike most books I have read on the subject. Its authors are equippers who have wrestled with this missionary question, who have trained others wrestling with it, and who continue to humbly live as learners of Jesus hoping to embody the missionary heart of our Father.

Read *Tradecraft*, but only if you are ready to be disoriented, to be challenged to abandon how you may have thought of missions, and to be reoriented to thinking and living like a missionary. In terms of theory, it defines those terms necessary for aligning ourselves with the same intent as Jesus' prayer in John 17. In terms of practice, it offers suggestions for living as answers to what Jesus prayed in John 17, all the while inviting you into a stealthy lifestyle of planting the gospel of the God who came near.

In fact, one of the many things that impresses me about these Upstream leaders is that they have not written this book so that you can fulfill a missionary duty. It is their hope that the lost and lonely of our world, whether they be right in your backyard or on the other side of the globe, might come to believe that they too are loved by the God who came near. It is also their hope, I believe, that we as the Church would quit doing missions, and instead be compelled by the Holy Spirit to be His missionaries. After all, that is the crux of mission: taking up the divine challenge to love others as we have been loved.

May we embody this love that is near, as we go and live among those we have been sent to encounter with the good news of Jesus. That will not happen unless and until we think of ourselves as missionaries in the way that Jesus saw Himself. This book helps us to do just that.

**Jason Dukes,**
Pastor of Westpoint Church in Orlando, FL, Founder of the Reproducing Churches Network & the Church at West Orange, and author of *Live Sent: You are a Letter* and *Beyond My Church.*

# PREFACE

BY RODNEY CALFEE

I am not a missionary.

I've never lived overseas or worked for a missions agency or had a postcard with my family's picture on it on anyone's refrigerator. I've never battled the jungles of a Third-World nation, braving untold danger to take the Gospel to a previously unreached native tribe. I've also never braved the urban jungle of a major global city, navigating all of its tribes and post-Christian sentiment for the sake of the Gospel.

I am from a mid-sized city in the heart of the Bible Belt, home to a culture shaped by college football, suburbia, and our finest export, cultural Christianity. With the number of mega-churches in my city, there is no need for more churches; at least, that's what I heard when I was a part of planting a new church 13 years ago. In fact, the majority of the people in my city would likely call themselves Christians. The *vast* majority.

Missionaries don't live here. Missionaries live where people haven't heard the Gospel. They live where it is dark and hard and liberal (the result of not understanding the Gospel according to many in my city), right? The South - the Christian South - doesn't need missionaries. There are churches on every corner. There is Christian music playing in many of our bookstores and cafes and skating rinks. If people want to "find God" there are a plethora of options just outside their doors. Isn't that enough?

I used to think so.

I thought, like so many others, that the problem people had with church was not the message, but the medium. Surely, if we created a space where we did all of the things we had done growing up in church, only cooler, lost people would turn to Jesus in droves. So, we gave it a shot. An entire generation of discontented believers did as well. And it worked, kind of. A lot of people like us who had left the church for various and sundry reasons returned. And some other people saw those people returning and joined them. Lost people. And they heard the Gospel and believed. Praise the Lord!

But what then?

Many were plugged into the same system I grew up in, one where we lived our lives working hard within the walls of the church and inviting our friends to come with us. I remember coaxing many a friend to my youth group with the promise of pizza, hot dogs, basketball, and leftover candy from the "Trunk-or-Treat." This generation is doing it again, except all of those things are for our kids now.

Don't get me wrong, I love that I grew up as a part of a church - a great church with wonderful people who genuinely wanted to see others follow Jesus. I am thankful for the numerous Sunday School teachers and children's choir directors and preachers and youth leaders who poured themselves into my life. I am thankful for my church. I am thankful that I came to know Christ at an early age and that I was taught to know him better over the years. I am thankful that I was taught to serve and love people because Jesus loved them. I am truly thankful.

There is, however, something I wish I had been taught that I wasn't. Maybe someone told me it was true at some point, but I don't remember, because it's not what I saw – what I *experienced* – as the norm growing up in church. I remember learning to pray, study my Bible, memorize Scripture, worship in song, fast, and many other wonderful and necessary disciplines. I learned a great deal about what I should do, but very little about who I *am*.

You see, I am a missionary. Right here. Right in my mid-sized city full of Bible-carrying, Scripture-misquoting, Jesus-fish-bumper-sticker-owning, God-and-Country-loving Southern American Christians. I'm not a missionary because of where of live. I am a missionary because of who I am, or more succinctly, because of who God has made me. I was a slave to sin, given over to the pleasures of the world. Jesus saved me and the old passed away. The new has come. I am a new creature in Christ; a new creature to whom Paul gives the name "ambassador" (2 Cor 5:17-21). That's my identity. I am a child of God, a co-heir with Christ, and a representative of my King and his Kingdom.

I am a man sent on a mission. It is God's mission, and is obviously far greater than me, but the mission defines me. I am a missionary.

I know that now, but I used to think differently. I thought differently because I continually saw and heard and believed that missions was somewhere "out there." Missionaries were the people we supported through special Christmas offerings who visited our churches and showed us slide shows of half-naked rural villagers and wowed us with the complexity of the languages they learned. They were the ones involved in mission.

14

I was a "layperson." I could evangelize, but somehow that was different than joining in God's mission. I could invite people to come hear professional missionaries or pastors or evangelists preach, but my main job was focused on me and my sanctification. I was a product of the same process that many of you were. And something is broken in that process, because, like me, you probably didn't (or don't) think of yourself as a missionary either. And that's sad, because, if you follow Jesus, you are following Him on mission, which makes you a missionary, too.

The system I experienced was hierarchical and divided. Within the church there were really three types of people: lay people, pastors or other church leadership, and missionaries. The higher in the hierarchy one went, the more committed he was. Christians were all meant to serve in the church, but there were those who were called out to serve as leaders. They became pastors and led the churches full of laypeople. They were committed, but the pinnacle of commitment came in the form of the missionary. The hierarchy looked something like this:

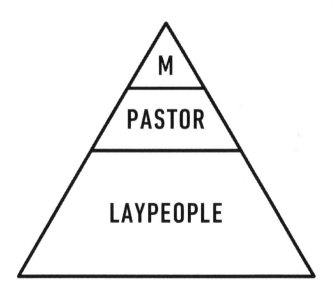

This model shaped a culture of hierarchy and privilege and a lack of identity for most who fell into the "Lay People" category. It also shaped a false sense of identity for those labeled pastors and missionaries. The laypeople began to look at them as superhero Christians, and the expectations placed upon them grew. So did the divide between them, causing a disconnect pushing missionaries apart from the rest of their churches. Missionaries began working together and (well-intentioned) agencies formed to enable missionaries to go to the people and places God was sending them. And it worked. Missionaries made their way across the globe and millions of people heard the Gospel and believed. Praise the Lord!

But as the divide continued to grow, missionaries became "Professional Christians," and churches turned over more and more of the responsibility for missions to agencies. Consequently, the missionary identity of all of God's people slipped further from their grasp and local churches lost sight of mission.

Churches became entrenched in this missions model, and it eventually became the norm. It has had far-reaching implications permeating all the way into the identities of believers. And it is a broken system.

Missions following this model might be diagramed in the following manner:

## THE PATHS TO MISSION

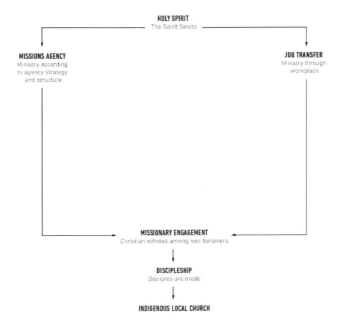

As you can see in the diagram of the traditional paths to mission, there are two ways to enter the field as a missionary. If an individual feels called to missions, he can either transfer through his employer or join a missions agency. Either path can land the missionary on the field and lead to missionary engagement, disciple-making, and indigenous church-planting. This method has worked. The process has grown more efficient over the years, and many have come to faith in Christ as a result. Praise the Lord!

So, what's the problem?

The problem is that there are now missionaries all over the world with virtually no connection to local churches to love and care for them, shepherd them, and join them on mission. There are also local churches full of laypeople talking about being "missional" without the benefit of learning from those who are actively crossing cultures with the Gospel. They are talking about mission without the input of missionaries.

We think there is a better way. We are thankful for the missionaries who have blazed the trail and the missions agencies which enabled them to go. We thank God for the work they have done and continue to do. However, we mourn the disconnect that has come as a result of the current missions model. We despise the fact that the Church has outsourced the Great Commission and removed herself from God's global mission on a grand scale; but we celebrate the recent growth in interest in and conversation around global mission, and we want to add to that conversation.

The Great Commission was given to the Church, and the Church (local churches) bears the responsibility for it. Parachurch ministries are an incredible gift to the Church, but only when they come alongside them as they are meant to do. Consider the following changes to the previous diagram:

## THE PATHS TO MISSION

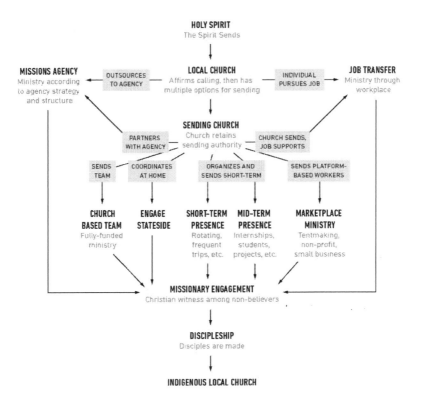

As you can see in this diagram, the local church retains the sending authority given by Jesus in the Great Commission. The traditional paths to mission still exist, but as two of many options for sending by the local church, not as "free agents" separate from the church. The church retains authority in the life of the ones who are sent and actually helps determine how engagement will happen. The missionaries, through the local sending church, are loved and shepherded, and the local church reaps the benefit of learning from the experience of the ones on the field.

As a result, the people within the local church become partners on the field and learn to think and act like missionaries both globally and locally. Their experience, through working alongside the ones they send out into international contexts will help them understand how to live out their own identities as ambassadors for Christ and His kingdom.

They will learn to be who they already are: missionaries. In their own cultures and contexts.

Remember the hierarchical diagram dividing laypeople from pastors and missionaries? Imagine that triangle dissolving and the divisions breaking down and forming one large pool of people all called "Missionaries." Some of the missionaries are gifted pastors and teachers and evangelists and apostles and prophets, and they lead the churches. Some missionaries are called to move to far-away lands. Other missionaries are gifted musicians and writers and lawyers and bankers and cooks and salesmen and landscapers who don't move across the globe. In fact, they may never leave their hometowns. They stay where they are and do the things for which they are gifted. But those things are just what they do by God's sovereignty. However, all of them are missionaries by His grace.

This is a better way.

As I mentioned earlier, I was part of planting a church in my city. I was a pastor in that church for more than a decade, and I never would have called myself a missionary. I had no idea what it meant to think and act like one. I didn't know I should. I was working in my city unaware of my own identity and the freedom and power that accompany it. Thankfully, there were some men kind enough and brave enough to point it out to me.

I am thankful that the other three authors of this book, whom I have the privilege of calling friends and co-laborers, came to my city and shared their stories with some friends and me. They came speaking a language that I didn't really understand but which resonated somewhere deep within me. It was the language of the missionary. It was my language, and one I wanted desperately to know. Their kindness toward me changed me, and it helped to shape the wonderful people I was privileged to pastor into missionaries, as well.

A couple of years later, I was able to join the Upstream team full-time to help others experience the same thing I did - to help them think and act like missionaries, which I am still learning to do.

This book is a resource designed to help missionaries along in that process. It is for pastors and plumbers, guitarists and accountants, professional athletes and full-time Christian workers.

Consider the words of the great preacher Charles Haddon Spurgeon:

If Jesus is precious to you, you will not be able to keep your good news to yourself; you will be whispering it into your child's ear; you will be telling it to your husband; you will be earnestly imparting it to your friend; without the charms of eloquence you will be more than eloquent; your heart will speak, and your eyes will flash as you talk of his sweet love. ***Every Christian here is either a missionary or an impostor.*** Recollect that. You either try to spread abroad the kingdom of Christ, or else you do not love him at all.[1]

We are all missionaries. You are a missionary, and our prayer is that the pages to follow will help to equip you as you walk in this grand identity. It is our great pleasure to share our stories with you here. May you be encouraged and challenged to walk worthy of the calling to which you have been called (Eph 4:1).

Grace and peace.

---

1 Spurgeon, "A Sermon and a Reminiscence." Emphasis mine.

# INTRODUCTION

[Chapter 1]

BY CALEB CRIDER

In the 2001 film *Spy Game*, master spy Nathan Muir, played by Robert Redford, trains his new apprentice, Tom Bishop, played by Brad Pitt, to think and act like a spy. With the wisdom of experience, Muir trains Bishop in the "tricks of the trade." To observe without being detected, gathering useful information while filtering out everything that isn't important. To talk your way into someone's confidence, because favors from "friends" may be your lifeline. Don't give out personal information, truthful or otherwise, because you'll have to keep your story straight in future interactions. Don't become too attached to those you've convinced to help you — known as assets — because feelings only cloud your judgment and give others power over you. The training montage only lasts a few minutes, but it serves as a great example of the foundational skills necessary to espionage that can only be passed on from one spy to another. This is tradecraft.

Tradecraft is the collection of knowledge that serves as the foundation of all artisan labor. The blacksmith maintains the strength of the material by plunging hot iron into cool water before re-heating the cooling metal. The cabinet maker uses a gauge rather than a tape to measure, because in woodworking, numbers rarely add up. The sailor can't help but notice the color of the sky at sunset; it forecasts the weather for the coming day. These are the skills that make the difference between mere workers and master craftsmen. The wisdom of experience informs everything that a tradesman does. This is why most trades require an apprenticeship.

From routine tasks like cooking and cleaning to more complex actions such as playing a musical instrument or using a computer, nearly everything we do requires a certain degree of skill. Fine motor skills allow us to move a pen across paper with enough control to form legible characters. Reasoning skills help us make thousands of decisions each day. Social skills make it possible to navigate relationships. Life requires skill.

As we go, we develop new skills along the way. The nervous 16-year-old novice driver who can't keep the car in his own lane eventually becomes so comfortable with driving that it becomes second nature. He begins to think he can safely talk on the phone, eat, and shave all at the same time during his commute to work. What once seemed so scary, so completely overwhelming to manage, now seems like child's play. As foundational skills are mastered, new skills can be learned; the basics help us learn how to learn new things. As we become more proficient, our ability to improvise increases. A skilled worker is able to adjust to different situations and remain true to his purpose.

The Christian life also requires skill. Reading and interpreting the Bible requires that one know a bit about the context of the scriptures. The conscious decision to deny one's self and follow Christ is a constant struggle that only becomes a habit through practice. Prayer, fasting, taking a day of rest – these are learned behaviors that do not come naturally to most of us. These skills are honed through instruction, and are fostered to familiarity through repetition. Someone who has mastered the skill teaches it to those who need to learn the skill. Jesus called this discipleship.

## The Great Divide

I had been a church planter in Western Europe for about six years when I began to realize just how great the divide was between churches and God's mission. Throughout the year, groups from various churches in the States would come to assist us in our ministry. For them, this was a "mission trip," but for us, it was real life. We wanted to treat them as peers -- a bit of fellowship, some mutual encouragement, and then go out and engage people in gospel conversations. But for the most part, the well-meaning participants on these trips were missiologically illiterate. They were incapable of participating in international mission in any meaningful way.

One Monday morning, we sent a group of American Christian college students to hang out at the local university to learn all they could about the spiritual climate on campus. We prayed together, divided the group into pairs, and sent them on their way. Of the six teams, two had trouble navigating the metro system and never even found the campus. Two teams played frisbee on the soccer field, not speaking to a single student the entire time. One team quickly put together a "survey" and approached random students to ask them spiritual questions. Because what little response they received was quite negative, this team was discouraged. None of the teams came back with any meaningful spiritual insight about national college students.

These groups were very good at doing what they were told. On previous trips, they had all painted fences, handed out blankets, and played games with children. For the duration of their ten-day stay, group members were perfectly happy to sleep on the floor, walk great distances, and feel generally out of place in this "foreign" environment.

But when it came to the reasons for doing these things, the whys of mission, most of them had no idea beyond some vague concept of "reaching people" and a performance-based sense of duty.

So when we asked these volunteers to go out and incarnate the gospel, they were at a loss as to what, exactly, that might mean and how, practically, to do that. They had no understanding of urban living, social tribes, or persons of peace. They had no experience gathering pertinent geographical, social, or spiritual information that might assist in church planting efforts. They were unfamiliar with the unchanging gospel, and fearful of culture. Worst of all, few had any sense of why they were participating in such a trip in the first place. Without basic missionary tradecraft, a Christian is incapable of moving beyond volunteerism into partnership in mission.

## Missionary Identity

The most underdeveloped basic Christian skills are those related to missionary thinking and practice.

For many Christians in the West, "missionary" is a profession that involves raising funds, moving to another country, eating questionable food, and telling people about Jesus. Of course, there's a long tradition of this sort of missionary, from William Carey's work in India to Lottie Moon's efforts in China to Nate Saint's engagement of native tribes in Ecuador. But mission is not about location, it's about identity. Because we are followers of a missionary God who has revealed Himself through the Missionary Son, mission is central to our identity as Christians.

Mission is not something we do, it's something we are. Early Church Fathers used the word "mission" to refer to the interaction between the persons of the Holy Trinity; the Father sends the Son, they send the Spirit. This most basic understanding of mission is referred to as the *Missio Dei*, the mission of God. In modern times, the word "mission" has been used in reference to God's purposes to extend this divine communion to humanity through Christ. From the beginning, God has revealed Himself to be a missionary God. Everything that He does is either sending or gathering.

What we know of God we know because He's revealed it to us, and He has revealed Himself as redeemer of humanity. It's His nature. As missiologist David Bosch wrote: "Mission is not primarily an activity of the church, but an attribute of God. God is a missionary God."[1] If our understanding of God is strictly biblical, we do not know the Father except as a missionary. Sure, He reveals Himself as Father, Creator, Judge, and King, but always with a mission.

Throughout history, God's interaction with humanity is unique in that He doesn't just speak to people, He sends them. Noah's mission was to save the animals and repopulate the earth.[2] Abraham was sent to a new place to begin a new nation of people through whom God would bless all people.[3] Moses was sent to lead the Hebrews out of slavery.[4] Even reluctant missionaries were sent – Joseph[5] and Daniel[6] were taken against their wills, Jacob was chased,[7] Jonah brought by fish.[8] All of these examples serve as part of God's mission. That these men were indeed sent isn't just inferred, God actually uses the language, "I'm sending you…" In every case, His interaction can be summed up as, "Go," and the purpose, "to be an agent of salvation."

Nowhere is this more clearly seen than in Christ Himself, the Son who was sent by the Father. In passages like John 14, Jesus makes it clear that to see Him is to see the Father who sent Him.[9] God incarnate is God on mission among us. He proclaimed Himself as the gospel and lived it out before our very eyes. Mission wasn't something He did, it's who He is. Bosch refers to this as Christ's "self-definition," and he argues that all of His followers shared that same "self-definition."

The first believers responded to the gospel like sleeper agents being activated. It was the same with Matthew,[10] Peter and Andrew,[11] and all who were present at Pentecost;[12] they heard God's voice and went.

---

1 Bosch, *Transforming Mission*, 389–390.

2 Genesis 9:1–29.

3 Genesis 12–17.

4 Genesis 3:1–12.

5 Genesis 37:12–36.

6 Daniel 1:1–21.

7 Genesis 32:1–32.

8 Jonah 1:1–17.

9 John 14:9.

10 Matthew 9:9.

11 Matthew 4:19-20.

12 Acts 2:41.

Their calling was to follow Jesus - to join Him on His mission. The various "commissions" in scripture are not optional activities for a select few Christ-followers, they are reminders that in Christ, we are all sent, and they knew it. They found their identity in their sentness.

It makes no sense to talk about our faith, our Savior, or even God outside the context of mission. Talk of mission ending should bewilder us. How will we know God apart from His mission? He hasn't revealed that to us. The church exists to organize God's people on mission. Without mission, there is no church and we have no meaningful connection to one another. God has established that our relationship to Him and to one another is in His mission to redeem the world.

So it's not just the professional missionaries who need to learn missionary skills. Every single follower of Christ needs to know how to relate to different people in order to be "ambassadors" of the kingdom here on earth.

Unfortunately, most of the missionary skills have been stripped out of discipleship. Pastors teach their churches to study the Bible, to lead their families in love, to give generously, and to serve with integrity. But they leave out such vital missionary as contextual exegesis, cross-cultural communication, and group discipleship. They don't teach their people to look for bridges and barriers to the gospel and to navigate them well. They assume that spiritually mature people know what they need to know in order to engage the world.

They don't.

Being a missionary requires skill. It's not something we're naturally good at. It takes practice to share our faith well, to deliberately leave our own cultures and comforts for the sake of making disciples across those boundaries.

## We are both "missionaries" and "nationals"

In the missions world, there is often a distinction made between "missionaries" – those who have been sent to deliberately cross cultural boundaries – and "nationals"– the people who are on the receiving end of gospel ministry. We are convinced, however, that Christians on mission need to recognize that each of us is both missionary *and* "national." That is, in Christ, we are sent ones, but we are also recipients of the good news.

This book is for Christians everywhere who see themselves as being strategically placed by God wherever they are. We write to address a longstanding trend in the Church away from missionary identity, but we acknowledge that the opposite extreme would be equally dangerous. When we think of ourselves strictly as "missionaries," we begin to think that cultural rules don't apply to us. We look for shortcuts in communication and discipleship, adopting pragmatic methodologies that are not common among "locals" and that we ourselves would never employ were we insiders. Ultimately, this neglects our responsibility to model for others what it would look like if they were to live as committed followers of Christ within their own cultural context.

The skills laid out in this book are useful for full-time Christian workers and stay-at-home moms, doctors and janitors, musicians and mathematicians. Some of them may apply more directly to one or the other at one moment and another the next, but they are applicable in some fashion across the board.

## Tricks of the Trade

In the following chapters, we're not going to focus on the importance of mission. We're not trying to convince you to be involved in mission. Instead, we will cover nine basic missionary skills, or tradecraft, that we believe are foundational to missionary thought and activity. These skills are commonly taught to international missionaries before they set out to foreign lands. But these are not "international missionary skills," they are necessary and vital for all churches to teach all believers everywhere and in every vocation, in the context of the local church.

Some of these skills are broadly assumed among mature believers, others seem to be altogether unknown. Maybe you live in the town you grew up in, maybe you've deliberately moved to live among people who are different from you for the sake of ministry. Whether you're in professional ministry or simply living a missional life, the application of these skills is vital to your church's obedience in participating in God's global mission.

We begin with a chapter on being Spirit-led, in which we look at how a church determines where and how – not if – God wants them to be involved in His global mission. Following statistics and strategies is the "the norm" in many missions circles, which may deny the role of the Holy Spirit in sending the Church. Should it not be our default setting to be obedience to the leadership of the Spirit, regardless of whether or not His plans fit our strategies and expectations? Such an alignment requires the missionary to have a continual communion with God as he discovers his path to mission. We will explore what it means to be Spirit-led from both a biblical and practical perspective, with the goal of showing that mission both begins and is sustained through the leadership of the Holy Spirit.

Upon arriving on a mission field, the first thing any missionary does is begin to get the lay of the land. We must orient ourselves with the geography, the social environment, and the spiritual climate. We do this through the missionary skill of mapping, which is simply collecting insight through observation and recording it for the sake of collaboration, planning, and prayer. This is how a missionary gains insight into who lives where in a city and how their various experiences affect their social and spiritual outlooks. Knowing and joining the people to whom you've been sent is the beginning of following Christ's example of incarnation. Mapping is a useful tool for the missionary entering a new city, as well as the missionary who begins to see his hometown as the place to which he is sent. Understanding social, economic, spiritual, and cultural boundaries is essential in any incarnational work, and cannot be overlooked by any missionary who hopes to effectively impact his community with the gospel.

As the missionary map is compiled, he can begin informed cultural exegesis. This is the process of finding the bridges and barriers to the communication of the gospel and beginning to answer the question of how the unchanging gospel truly is "good news" to the people you serve. The Apostle Paul modeled this missionary behavior for us; every culture and subculture retains some echoes and shadows of God's Truth. Cultural exegesis is the missionary exploration of a culture from a Kingdom perspective. These things can be subtle: the upkeep of property, for example, gives us insight into the demographics of a neighborhood. Parsing of local legends and mythologies can show the true beliefs of a people group. A good look at social structures can reveal the idols worshiped by a segment of the population. Appropriate gospel ministry to any group requires this skill. Without an understanding of the people he is sent to, a missionary cannot effectively incarnate the gospel as good news to them, because he doesn't understand how it is good news to them.

Cultural exegesis can be done to some extent from afar, but its purpose is to help the missionary get "close" to the people he is learning about. The point of learning the culture is to learn how the people think and live in order to build relationships with them. Relationships are the means by which incarnational ministry is carried out, and building relationships is not always an easily accomplished task, particularly for outsiders. All Christians are by nature outsiders, because we give allegiance to a different kingdom and King and hold a vastly different worldview than "the world." Building relationships with non-believers, then, requires particular skill, whether the missionary is in his home culture or halfway around the world. There must be some basis in order for conversations of profound spiritual nature to take place. Stories with such deep meaning must be built on a solid foundation. That foundation is relationship, and the missionary must be devoted to building relationships well, if he intends to share something so intensely personal and overtly objective as the gospel. Avoiding proper relationships can lead to either deep misunderstanding and outright rejection of the gospel or a "bait and switch" of sorts that leads to distrust and can ruin the opportunity he may have had to share the gospel with someone. Therefore, building relationships is of the highest importance for a missionary, and for many, it is a very difficult skill to develop.

Although building relationships can be quite difficult, there is someone who can help apart from, of course, the Holy Spirit. We just have to find him in our particular contexts. Have you ever wondered what it would be like to have an audience with the President? Or to hang out over coffee with your favorite movie star? Or lunch with a lifelong sports hero? Have you ever actually tried to make it happen? For most of us, it is next to impossible, at best. Unless, of course, we "know" someone. If, by chance, you know someone who knows the booking agent of your favorite rock star and you somehow bribe them into giving you his schedule for the day, you may actually be able to go to coffee with him (just before the police show up). Without some sort of connection, though, most of us would just be out of luck.

In real life, connections can be wonderful things, and connectors are infinitely valuable people. In His instructions to the disciples He sent on a short-term mission trip, Jesus spoke of individuals who had been divinely prepared beforehand to open doors to other people into their social circles. He refers to these people as "persons of peace." Finding these insiders can be invaluable to the efforts of a missionary as he works in and among the people to whom he is called. The ability to identify such people and walk with them into new relationships is a tool that greatly builds the capacity of a missionary.

Often with the help of the person of peace, the missionary is able to identify and even be welcomed into certain social circles, namely the person of peace's tribe. The ability to recognize and gain entry into certain social and relational circles is imperative for the missionary. Church planting among unbelievers can be like finding a seat in the high school cafeteria. The majority of the people we meet are already connected in tightly-knit social circles that serve to help make sense of the world around them. These tribes have largely replaced family, clan, and ethnic groupings as a person's primary social influence. Some might see the existence of these groups, with their unwritten rules, fuzzy boundaries, and nuanced differences as being a barrier to the spread of the good news. The missionary, however, sees these naturally-formed groups not as barriers, but as opportunities to see the gospel take root in an indigenous way. He sees churches waiting to happen. Therefore, the ability to recognize and gain entry into tribes is a non-negotiable tool as he goes on mission.

Ultimately, the ability of the sent Christian to communicate the gospel into culture in any meaningful way requires the skill of contextualization. This is the work of translating the gospel from one culture into another. It is the ability of the believer to make the unchanging gospel make sense in ever-changing and diverse cultures. The need for contextualization is most clearly seen in terms of language: the missionary must see to it that the message of Christ is communicated in a language that is understood by his audience. But context extends beyond language to worldview: religion, identity, history, and socio-economic status. Good contextualization requires skill, lest we lose the gospel in cultural obscurity or familiarity.

Understanding and engaging the cultural context of the people to whom you are sent requires finding bridges into relationships in contextually appropriate ways. Whether it be in a new culture in a distant land or your hometown, there are traditional pathways to relationships in both places. Local churches tend to work through services, outreach programs, special events and other such tools to relate to the community around them. Those things can be effective, but the decline in church attendance in the US over the past several decades says that the reach of those tools is shrinking. There is, however, a growing trend - and rightly so - toward alternative paths through which the common everyday missionary can work through natural, pre-existing groups of people. The workplace, school, the playground, the grocery store, and a neighborhood athletic field are all places where community is built. Missionaries recognize those places as being ready-made petri dishes for relational growth. In the same manner, the most common path into a foreign culture has been through "missionary" status as a full-time Christian worker. Alternative paths into those cultures are becoming increasingly important.

Many countries are closed to the gospel, so access requires an alternative reason for being there. There are other cultures that are not necessarily "closed" to the gospel, but certainly indifferent toward the Christian worker, at best. They either do not understand why the missionary is there, or resent his presence altogether, making the relational connections necessary for gospel transmission incredibly difficult to build. If the missionary enters a culture with a similar reason for being there as the nationals, then relational barriers that would have been created through "missionary" status are avoided. The most common way for the missionary to accomplish this is through work. By producing something that adds to the community around him and provides a means to earn a living, the missionary is more likely able to become a real part of the community. He will also provide a natural means for finding and developing relationships through his work. Recognizing alternative paths into mission is a tool in desperate need of development among missionaries.

As relationships flourish and opportunities to share the gospel yield fruit, new believers begin to emerge. The natural question that follows is what to do with those new disciples. Do you find an existing local body and integrate them into it? Do you start something new? If so, what should it look like? Imagine what church plants in San Francisco, New York, Atlanta, Nashville, New Delhi, Hong Kong, and Istanbul look like. Do you have a picture in your mind? In what ways should those churches be alike? How should they be different? The Great Commission does not say go into the world and plant churches or simply start creative worship services. It says "go into the world and make disciples." When we go into the world and plant churches we tend to make them look like the churches that we come from. After all, our pragmatism leads us to believe that if it can work at home then it can work anywhere. But this attitude overlooks the missionary skill of protecting indigeneity. The result of our work should be biblical, local, independent churches that reflect the soil in which they are planted. What if our attempts at recreating what works at home in other parts of the world are not only ineffective but harmful when it comes to reproducing disciples?

Missionary tradecraft are the tools that make it possible for you to do what you were made to do. Practice them until they become second nature, and you will be equipped to do ministry in any context. Our hope is that by mastering these skills, your church will learn to think and act like the missionary it is meant to be.

This list of skills is by no means exhaustive. There are many, many more to be learned and employed. The skills we have chosen to expound upon in the pages to follow are basic, important, practical, and relatively unknown.

## All Christians On Mission

The content of this book may sound similar to other international missions resources out there. This is due to the fact that we're reapplying international missionary skills to Christian lifestyle ministries everywhere. But if some of what we've written here sounds familiar on the front end, it will likely seem less familiar as you progress into each chapter. We have made deliberate adjustments to the concepts treated here, to make them more clear, biblical, and applicable to the local church.

In fact, some of what we've written here is the opposite of what you might hear from the traditional missions world. In our chapter on being Spirit-led, for example, we don't assume you've been called to serve among an unreached people group. When we outline the concept of the person of peace as it's found in Luke 10, we're sure to point out that finding this person can be as much a distraction as a help. We've gathered ideas, synthesized them, and applied them in ways their original proponents may not have. Our goal is not to blindly promote innovation or to be contrary, but to help churches think and act like missionaries at home and internationally.

We suspect that some in the missions world will resent the fact that we're sharing freely what is usually reserved only for the professionals. Our chapters on mapping and indigeneity certainly wade into the territory of missions schools and agencies. But we firmly believe that the time has come to end the distinction between "missions" and "home ministry." We want to make missions resources available to Christians everywhere so that they can become the missionaries they were saved to be.

As we embark on the journey of exploring missionary skills, we invite you to wrestle through the application of these skills in your own context. Whether you're serving in East Asia or West Virginia, we believe that these skills will radically affect how you obediently engage the people around you with the gospel of Jesus Christ.

# FOLLOWING THE SPIRIT

## [Chapter 2]

BY LARRY E. MCCRARY

## The Tale of Two Churches

Joshua is a young church planter in an urban area in the United States. He and his wife planted a church a mere two years after graduating from college. A small group of their college friends comprised the core leadership group. From those modest beginnings, the church grew rapidly, adding mainly young adults and families, most of whom had little or no church background.

Currently, the church holds multiple services in a rented facility one day a week. They have been involved in a few community mission projects, and they are supporting a couple of other local church plants. At this time they do not have any overseas projects or partners. However, Joshua realizes if they are going to fully embrace the Great Commission and Acts 1:8, they must become involved globally. He knows they should be involved and wants to know how they get started on mission.

Shawn is the mission pastor of another church in the same city that has experienced exponential growth in the last four years. The suburban church has multiple campuses and utilizes video technology for teaching on several of the campuses. They have campus pastors for each site, but they manage all of their ministries and staffing from one central location.

Shawn and his wife started attending the church when it first began. He had a passion for missions and even served overseas for a two-year stint. As the church grew, he naturally became the point person for missions. Eventually, the pastor asked him to join the staff as the mission leader in the church.

Because there was no real direction for the missions thrust within the church from the beginning, mission programs just popped up as people wanted to be involved somewhere. As a result, the missions ministry of the church never had a distinct focus. The church now partners with numerous local and global ministries, but it appears that each member develops his own mission strategy and then tries to get the church involved.

If you list all of their activities on a white board, the result is an impressive number of mission endeavors. Even so, Shawn's desire is to lead the church beyond simply sending money to its partnerships and outsourcing the Great Commission. He wants to move beyond only leading short-term trips around the world. His goal is to pare down the amount of places in which they work to a few strategic partnerships with which they are deeply involved. He, like Joshua, is looking for a starting point in the process.

## Common Strategies

As I think about how churches strategize their mission endeavors, these two churches exemplify a common situation among churches. Joshua's church is starting from scratch. They have a blank page on which to begin sketching out how they will go on mission. Shawn, in quite the opposite situation, is working to turn a confusing conglomeration of projects into a sensible and focused long-term investment in mission. He is trying to decide what to de-emphasize so that he can make sense of the mission work of his church.

Interestingly enough, both of these churches need to be asking the same questions—"to whom" and "to where" are we sent? These questions will offer clarity and direction to the church with a blank page as well as to the church attempting to wade through a sea of disconnected and directionless programs. A plethora of methodologies have been developed for determining the answers to these questions over the years of missionary endeavors. The range of criteria is vast, and each strategy has been developed out of a heart to fulfill the Great Commission. Here are a few noteworthy examples

• **Focus on the 10/40 window**—The Joshua Project defines the 10/40 window as "the rectangular area of North Africa, the Middle East, and Asia approximately between 10 degrees north and 40 degrees north latitude. The 10/40 Window is often called "The Resistant Belt" and includes the majority of the world's Muslims, Hindus, and Buddhists.[1] In many cases you will hear this term used interchangeably with World A peoples or Last Frontier.

• **Focus on the least reached peoples**—The rationale of this approach centers on not going where the gospel has already gone. As many people have stated, "Why should anyone hear the gospel twice until all have had the chance to hear it once?" Churches should instead go to the people who have never heard. Missiologist Gordon Olson says, "If we have a choice and unless there are compelling reasons to the contrary, the Christian worker should

---

1 Joshua Project, "What is the 10/40 Window?"

choose the place of greatest need! Failure to give adequate consideration to this factor has caused the incredible inequity in the distribution of workers."[2] As such, emphasis on Unreached People Groups (UPGs – a homogeneous population group identified by a common language, heritage, and religion with no church movement having sufficient strength, resources, and commitment to sustain and ensure the continuous multiplication of churches)[3] or Unengaged Unreached People Groups (UUPGs – UPGs with the added element of no known missionary engagement with the particular people group) should be given strategic priority.

• **Focus on large urban centers of over 100,000 in population where fewer than two percent of the people are evangelized** — Some missiologists suggest that people who live in rural areas come to the city to live and work, but they travel back to their villages or small towns several times a year. Therefore, if missionaries focus their efforts on the cities, then new believers who come to Christ in the city can take the gospel back to their homes in the outlying areas.

• **Invest in local church planters or pastors**—In some case local believers already know the culture and the language, and they are already connected relationally to their culture and people, whereas cross-cultural missionaries must learn those things and build relationships from the ground up. The idea behind this strategy is that it makes more sense to invest in these local church planters, because they can most quickly and efficiently take the gospel to their own people groups.

• **Invest in near-culture church planters or pastors**—If there are no Christians within a given people or culture group, the next best thing is to have someone who is part of the closest culture to theirs go to them. While near-culture missionaries are not from the unreached people group, they do live near or even among them already. They are already familiar with the cultural context and can get to the gospel presentation and church plant quicker.

---

2 Olson, *What in the World is God Doing?*, 86.

3 International Mission Board, "Glossary."

Again, all of these approaches have the intent to fulfill the Great Commission and can be useful tools for the church on mission. While we can learn from effective strategies, we must determine the source of our direction in mission. There are so many varying strategies that a church would be taking a shot in the dark to choose between them. The tools are just not enough; they do not stand on their own.

## How Do We Know?

In reality, even when offered a list of engagement strategies, the church still faces questions: How do we decide where to engage? Which strategy is right for us? Do we look at programs, strategies, and statistics and base our decision on research?

More importantly, churches should be asking more basic questions such as: What does Scripture have to say on how we develop our mission strategy? Aren't we supposed to be following the Spirit? The decision involves more than choosing from a list of strategies or missions organizations.

Missionary and author Lesslie Newbigin in his classic book *The Open Secret* wrote,

> My own experience as a missionary has been that the significant advances of the church have not been the result of our own decisions about mobilizing and allocating of 'resources.' The significant advances in my experience have come through happenings of which the story of Peter and Cornelius is a paradigm, in ways of which we have no advance knowledge. God opens the heart of a man or woman in the gospel.[4]

The story Newbigin refers to is found in Acts 10 and centers on God leading Peter to Cornelius by way of His Spirit. There is no strategic attempt on Peter's part to evangelize Cornelius. In fact, quite the opposite exists. Peter's "strategy" did not include the Gentiles. Therefore, apart from the Spirit's leadership, Peter's strategy would have fallen short of where God wanted the gospel to go. In the same way, while contemporary strategies can be useful tools, they may fall short or

---

4 Newbigin, *The Open Secret*, 64.

even lead us to the wrong places or keep us out of a place God wants us to go.

## Jesus Gave Us a Gift

The Acts 10 account is far from the only time we see the Holy Spirit as the sending agent in the Scriptures. We also hear of the role of the Spirit in mission from Jesus himself:

And Jesus came and said to them, "All authority in heaven and on earth has been given to me. Go therefore and make disciples of all nations, baptizing them in the name of the Father and of the Son and of the Holy Spirit, teaching them to observe all that I have commanded you. And behold, I am with you always, to the end of the age" (Matt. 28:18–20).

The authority Jesus received for His mission came from God the Father. However, Jesus passed this responsibility and authority on to us. The agent, again—the direction and strength for sending—was the Spirit. Jesus said to them again, "Peace be with you. As the Father has sent me, even so I am sending you." And when he had said this, he breathed on them and said to them, "Receive the Holy Spirit" (John 20:21–22).

In his classic book, *The Master Plan of Evangelism*, Robert Coleman wrote, "The initial objective of Jesus' plan was to enlist men who could bear witness to His life and carry on His work after He returned to the Father."[5] His point is that our missionary endeavors are not solely ours. The mission is God's. As He led and gave authority to Christ, we have been given authority and the leadership of the Spirit (2 Tim. 2:2).

In the Matthew 28:18-20 passage referenced above, Jesus assured His followers that they would not go on mission alone. He promised He would be with them as they went. He promised the same thing in Acts 1, but with a twist: "But you will receive power when the Holy Spirit has come upon you, and you will be my witnesses in Jerusalem and in all Judea and Samaria, and to the end of the earth" (Acts 1:8). The power to "be witnesses" came from the indwelling Spirit. God was with them as He sent them out on mission giving them authority, direction, and strength for the missionary life ahead.

---

5 Coleman, *The Master Plan of Evangelism*, 21–22.

## It's Spiritual

What we see, then, is that strategy is not enough. There is a spiritual element required before a useful strategy can ever be developed, much less employed. That spiritual direction comes only via a close communion with God through Scripture, prayer, and intentional listening to his voice. Pastor and author John Piper wrote on discerning the specific calling of God on one's life. The same can be applied to the missionary call and involvement of a local church, as well:

First, I suggest that you give yourself to the word of God. Immerse yourself in God's assessment of you and the world, so that you see things through God's eyes. Secondly, get a realistic view of yourself —your gifts, weaknesses, and strengths—and let others help you by participating in the Body of Christ and having them comment on what things they see in you. Third, look at the situation in the world, either in your immediate vicinity or in some distant place, and get a burden for the world.[6]

As Piper points out, common sense is a part of discerning our missionary call. Understanding who we are and the gifts God has given us impact deeply the role we play in mission. But much more exists. I like how Piper connects his practical advice with the spiritual; "stirring them together with the stirring spoon of prayer can give us a clear sense of direction."[7] There is a spiritual aspect, something supernatural and beyond our control. That is the work of the Holy Spirit. Again, our missional endeavors are not on our own, they are God's. And as such, God is guiding us by His Spirit.

The Holy Spirit supernaturally convicts the world of sin and gives us boldness, courage, and comfort as we go on mission.[8] The Spirit is also our guide along the way (Rom. 8:14; Gal. 5:18, 25). As such, theologian Wayne Grudem defines the work of the Holy Spirit as "manifest[ing] the active presence of God in the world, and especially in the church."[9]

---

6 Piper, "How Can I Discern the Specific Calling of God on My Life?"

7 Ibid.

8 John 16:7–8, 14:26; Acts 4:31, 9:31.

9 Grudem, *Systematic Theology*, 634.

Jesus emphasized the role of the Spirit in leading the disciples after His departure, saying, "But the Helper, the Holy Spirit, whom the Father will send in my name, he will teach you all things and bring to your remembrance all that I have said to you." And: "When the Spirit of Truth comes, he will guide you into all truth" (John 14:26; 16:13a). He taught that the Spirit would bear witness about Him and pick up the role of leader in the leadership vacuum left in Jesus' absence.

In short, the Holy Spirit leads us on mission. God, by way of His indwelling Spirit, is our authority through Christ. Paul's direction for us is that we should be in step with the Spirit, which implies step-by-step leadership (Gal. 5:25). Therefore, our direction for missionary engagement comes from the Spirit. Though strategies can be useful tools, we should not automatically default to mere statistics or felt needs to discern our call in mission. Our answer to the "where" and the "to whom" questions should not simply be the latest mission program or idea. Instead, it should be the result of a deep and intentional attentiveness to the leadership of the Spirit.

Caleb Crider, co-founder of The Upstream Collective, often reminds us that "our necessary dependence on the step-by-step leadership of the Holy Spirit is often an afterthought in mission. We tend to consult Him once, then ask for His blessing on our strategy rather than allow Him to guide our every turn along the way. Our mission depends on the Holy Spirit's guidance every step of the way."[10]

Martyn Lloyd-Jones, the late theologian and pastor of Westminster Chapel in London, said of the Holy Spirit's leading, "Here again is a most extraordinary subject, and indeed a very fascinating one, and, from many angles, a most glorious one. There is no question but that God's people can look for and expect 'leadings,' 'guidance,' 'indications of what they are meant to do.'"[11] It is curious, then, that our tendency as local churches and mission agencies is to subscribe, sometimes blindly, to a prescribed strategy without a constantly listening and discerning ear tuned into the voice of our Lord. That begs the question, "What happens when God wants us to do something or go somewhere outside the norm of our philosophical or anthropological strategy (as He did with Peter in Acts 10)?"

---

10 The Upstream Collective, *The Upstream Collective Jet Set Vision Trip Guidebook, 2011*, 30.

11 Lloyd-Jones, *The Sovereign Spirit*, 89–90.

## A Pattern in Scripture

In Acts 8, the Spirit sent out Phillip from a city into a deserted area. He was simply told to go south along the road. He obeyed. A chariot came into view carrying an Ethiopian official who was reading the book of Isaiah. The Spirit instructed Phillip to join the official, and he again obeyed. With each step of obedience an opportunity came for Phillip to listen and act accordingly for the Spirit's guidance.

Interestingly, the Spirit was also at work in the life of the Ethiopian official. He, a Gentile, was returning home from worshipping in Jerusalem and was reading Isaiah—quite an anomaly in and of itself. Led by the Spirit, Phillip was able to ask the official if he understood what he was reading, which opened the door for him to share the good news of Jesus with the official. Phillip's obedience to the Holy Spirit's very strange leading gave him opportunity to have a gospel conversation with the Ethiopian who believed and was baptized. Again, this was outside the normal strategy of the early Church at this point, which was preaching only to the Jews.

Another story recorded in the book of Acts is commonly referred to as the "Macedonian call" and occurred during Paul's second missionary journey. On his first journey, Paul had a very pragmatic approach. He would enter a city, preach in the synagogues, deal with the responses appropriately, and move on to the next city (Acts 13–14). Apparently, he began his second journey in the same fashion (Acts 16:4), but the Spirit frustrated his attempts along the way.

Paul was "forbidden by the Holy Spirit to speak the word in Asia" (Acts 16:6), even though that region was full of unreached people who had never heard the gospel. Then when Paul's team attempted to go into Bithynia, "the Spirit of Jesus did not allow them" (Acts 16:7). Finally, the Spirit led Paul by way of a dream in which a man called him to go and help the people of Macedonia. Paul immediately changed his course and obeyed the Spirit's leading.

Paul wrote to the Romans (15:20) that the strategy he practiced was to preach where no one else had—where the name of Christ was not known. However, he obediently strayed from his pragmatism when the Spirit led. If the Spirit were to forbid us from doing something as essential to our mission as preaching the Word to a given people, would we do it? If He prevented us from meeting some obvious need, would we recognize it as Him? Are we willing to accept "no" as an answer from the Lord? I would personally like to say I have this figured out but

I do not. Too often, I have a hard time accepting a "no" or "redirection." I have to stay attuned to what the Spirit is saying to me, which requires a constant communion with my Savior.

Scripture records a very simple pattern of listening and obeying when it comes to following the Holy Spirit. In story after story, an individual receives direction, a calling, or prompting by the Spirit. Then the faithful hearer responds in obedience. This is a critical pattern for a church determining the who, what, when, and where of mission.

Again, Newbigin, speaking of the root causes of great historical advances of the Church in mission, offered insight on this subject. He wrote, "It was not part of any missionary strategy devised by the church. It was the free and sovereign deed of God, who goes before His church. And, like Peter, the church can usually find good reasons for being unwilling to follow. But follow it must if it is to be faithful. For the mission is not ours but God's."[12]

## My Story

In 1988, my wife Susan and I attended a mission conference in Chattanooga, Tennessee. Susan was playing violin with the orchestra during the conference that night. I was in my spot-of-choice in the auditorium, the back row. To be perfectly honest I was only there to listen to her play the violin. I had never really considered missions as a vocation. However, at the end of the session, the speaker challenged us to respond to the call to missions by coming forward to the platform. Surprisingly, we responded independently of one another and met unexpectedly at the front. Thus began our missions journey which first played itself out as we were part of planting eight churches here in the United States.

After working with church plants for ten years in the United States, we sensed God leading us to turn our attention overseas. I was a little ahead of my wife on this idea. She had recently been on a short-term mission trip to Chile with our church. While she was on the trip, I sensed God wanted us to be open to going overseas. She, on the other hand, believed God was leading us to continue in missions but in North America.

Either way, we knew change was coming. We had to open our hearts and minds to the possibilities ahead. I needed to be open to

---

12 *The Open Secret*, 64.

other places in North America, and Susan admitted that she needed to "pray about praying about" going overseas. So, we continued to read Scripture and pray together while confiding in a few close friends.

Our son was a preschooler at the time. We decided to put a large map of the world on his bedroom wall. I am sure we told him just how cool it was to have a map of the world on his wall. His room became the place where we would go to pray, learn geography, and wonder together about where God might be leading us.

I remember that as we started to process our calling with other people, many interesting opinions about where we should serve began to surface. We were told that we did not need to go to South America, because the gospel had already taken root there and missionaries were no longer needed. Another person told us that Europe was not a valid option either. Since the gospel had already been there, it would be way too easy.

As we began to digest what other people were telling us, a question surfaced: What if God asked us to do something that may not make sense? What if He asked us to go somewhere and do something that defied simple logic? We were overwhelmed with strategies and did not want to miss God's voice in the midst of them.

## Pragmatism Breeds Models

Many people struggle with these same questions because of a basic and innate desire for pragmatism. By default, we tend to value what works. If a given model works, then God must be blessing it; and it must be the "right way" to do it. A stroll through the local Christian bookstore reveals our pragmatic bent. The successful pastor/missionary/ Christian entrepreneur/youth worker/church planter writes a book outlining exactly how he achieved success in his field. It becomes an instant best-seller, because everyone hoping to be successful in the same field immediately buys the book and implements the steps. A church model is born.

Models are a staple in missional engagement. Some mission strategists believe we should go only where there is an obvious harvest. Others say the determining factor is actually the speed of results. In some cases, we actually see both of these rationales combined.

For example, I was talking with a church several years ago about partnering with us in Western Europe. The church was set to come over and implement some creative mission initiatives. Mere months before their scheduled visit, however, I received a phone call letting me know they needed to put the partnership on hold. The pastor said the church had adopted a plan to see one person come to Christ for every member of the church that year. They had about 1500 members, giving them a very robust goal.

The pastor communicated their need to evaluate their ministries and place maximum effort in those initiatives that would potentially produce the most harvest. Since Western Europe is not a current harvest field, they needed to reallocate their missions efforts into more obviously fruitful places. Although they originally believed the Lord had led them to partner in Western Europe, pragmatism won the day and ultimately shaped their missionary focus.

If something draws a crowd who might actually listen to us, is it always good? What if God leads us to do something that does not quickly, or ever, produce visible results? A definitive tension exists here – "what works" versus "what we are called to." They may not necessarily be the same thing. Something may have worked for another person because it was what God led him to do. The simple fact that it worked for him doesn't make it the default strategy for everyone else. In the beginning, we need to forget strategies; our only guide for mission is the Holy Spirit.

## Back to Our Personal Journey . . .

Conventional missionary wisdom and strategy told my wife and me to go to Asia or Africa—to be real missionaries. But the Spirit was leading us in another direction. As we prayed, studied Scripture, and took a good look at our own gifts and ministry experience, God showed us His direction for us.

Even though strategies would have sent us elsewhere, we sensed God leading us to Europe, a post-Christian context that many churches and organizations write off as "reached." Europe was home to the Reformation, after all, and the Church deeply influenced the culture there for centuries. Because of that fact, many say Europe does not need missionaries. However, we sensed the Lord asking us to work toward spiritual renewal in Europe. We did not think we were the end-all-and-be-all Christian workers who would ignite revival and save all of Europe. We felt we just needed to be a part of what God was doing there. The Holy Spirit guided us step-by-step through the entire process.

It was a case of the Holy Spirit practical versus pragmatic practical. Here is what the process looked like for our twisting, winding path in the journey. We:

- prayed;
- researched European countries and cities;
- began to build relationships with people who lived there;
- took a vision trip to Europe;
- prayed more;
- studied Scripture and asked God for wisdom and guidance;
- asked a small group of people in our local church to pray with us;
- involved our pastors in conversations early on and throughout the process;
- prayed more;
- researched various sending agencies;
- assessed our own gifts;
- considered our children and their ages;
- assessed other Christian work in European cities;
- continued to pray.

After several months of prayer, Scripture study, and attentive listening, it became clear to us exactly where God wanted us to plant our lives for a season. He led us to Europe; and He continues to lead us by His spirit as we work there now.

## The Church Is Spirit-led

Our personal journey into missions is an example of being Spirit-led and is applicable to churches, not just individuals. Well-publicized strategy practices, statistical data, or catchy programs often influence churches. None of those things are inherently bad, but they should never supersede or usurp the role of the Holy Spirit.

Acts 13 contains an excellent example of how the Spirit directly led the church into mission. As was common, the church in Antioch was gathered together, praying, fasting, and worshipping the Lord. They were in close communion with God who spoke to them by way of the Holy Spirit: "Set apart for me Barnabas and Saul for the work to which I have called them" (Acts 13:3).

The Spirit spoke and gave the church very specific directions, which they obeyed. It was a very significant moment, because until this point in Scripture, a person's call seemed to be more individual. Think about Abram, Moses, Joshua, Isaiah, the disciples, etc. Each of these men had a specific call from God and usually for a certain task. But in Acts 13, the calling came within the context of community. The Spirit, who indwelled the believers, united them with one another; and in community, the Spirit guided the church in the specifics of missionary engagement.

# CHARACTERISTICS OF SPIRIT-LED CHURCHES: HOW-TO

As a part of my role with the Upstream Collective, I spend a great deal of time with North American pastors and in their churches. I have observed three common characteristics among those who demonstrate a Spirit-led approach to mission. Regardless of model, worship style, age of the church, or it's demographic, these characteristics exist in Spirit-led churches.

1. The church has a close communion with God. That may seem obvious, but it pervades their culture. They regularly and consistently pray, fast, study, listen, and learn together. They put into practice the direction God gives them together. They do not default to simple pragmatism. Often the result is a methodology that actually seems counter to the common practices of North American churches in mission.

2. The entire church understands its call to the nations. Mission defines whom this church is as opposed to being merely a program competing for budget dollars and time on the platform. The teaching of the church always keeps in mind the missionary purpose of the church, so that mission shapes the cultural identity of every person involved in the church.

3. The leadership is highly motivated and committed to seeing missions implemented in the church, both globally and locally. They model mission in their city and around the world, and they develop the vision into a workable strategy for the church. Mission then influences and shapes every ministry area and program of the church.

Our experience with Spirit-led churches points to a common decisive moment in which they realize God is calling them to a certain place or people based on His leadership. Just as Phillip was led step-by-step into his conversation with the Ethiopian eunuch, Spirit-led churches follow the same step-by-step leadership. The following are a few examples of the Spirit's leadership for churches in mission.

**Bill Jessup**, while pastor of Stafford Baptist Church in Stafford, Virginia, was watching The Discovery Channel several years ago and stumbled across a show about Iceland. As he watched the show, he sensed the Lord prompting him to lead his church to engage in Iceland and developed an immediate heart for the people there. He began sharing what God had shown him with his church and even approached a mission organization to begin a conversation about going. He finally determined that he needed to go to Iceland, which he did. During his visit he sensed the Lord confirming the call for Stafford to engage in Iceland. They engaged and sent short-term teams to develop relationships with the locals in Reykjavik, which eventually led to mid-term stints and two families who have moved there on a more permanent basis, including Jessup.

**Kyle Goen** was the executive pastor at Lifepoint Church in Smyrna, Tennessee. He and several others within the church participated in a few short-term trips to Brussels, Belgium. As they prayed and engaged in several ministry projects in the city, they started sensing God wanted them to have a more incarnational presence there. Eventually, the Lord used those trips, along with subsequent prayer and study with his church family to prompt Goen to move his family to Brussels and lead a church-planting team from Lifepoint Church to work there.

**A church in Florida** sensed the Lord leading them to work among Chinese people, but not in China. As they began to talk and pray about this within their church body, several people emerged who had relationships and connections within a Latin American country. After much prayer, the church determined that God was leading them to this particular country to work among Chinese immigrants there.

**Snow Hill Baptist Church**, just outside of Oklahoma City, Oklahoma, wanted to take its first step towards missionary engagement. One of Upstream's leaders spent a weekend with them to help them determine how they might proceed. During the weekend, a group of people within the church began to talk about where they might go. They came to a common conclusion in prayer. They pulled out their laptops and spent a couple of hours searching the Internet and gleaning as much as they could about the place they felt called to go.

Then, they gathered in prayer again, and sensed God giving them further direction about exactly where they should go.

I worked with a church, home to many international adoptive families, who began to realize that many of their children were from the same region of the world. Through prayer, they sensed God leading them to continue the work He had already begun —using their people to influence that area of the world for the sake of the gospel. They immediately began developing key partnerships in there.

I have also seen churches take a look at their community. They noticed that people from this particular restricted-access nation lived all around them. They knew that they should not go overseas to try to connect with this people while ignoring those whom God had placed before them. They concluded God was calling them to work with these people in the United States and then connect globally with them later on.

Once a church zeros in on where it should be involved then often the right opportunities start to emerge. I believe the Spirit will lead the church as it lives out the Great Commission in its community and abroad. It will soon start thinking and acting as a missionary.

During the weeks I have been working on this chapter I was talking to a young church planter who is preparing to plant a church in three months. He did not start by giving me the catchy name of the church or how he would brand the church. He did not start off by talking about the public launch. He did not go into the model of church or the worship style the church would have on Sunday morning. Instead he described for me what he wants the church to look like. Simply put, they want to be about making disciples wherever they are. He desires that as a church they will take seriously the characteristics of what happened in the church in Acts 13 where the people prayed and fasted and knew what they were to do. They would be faithful to the gospel. They would take God at His Word and obey Him step by step. They would send people out into their community, nation, and world as He leads. This is the pathway to mission.

# MAPPING

[Chapter 3]

BY CALEB CRIDER

Getting lost can be a difficult and frustrating experience. Any time we find ourselves in unfamiliar territory, we experience stress. We naturally look for anything that might help us figure out where we are. Signs help, assuming you're in a place where you can read them. Asking for directions may seem like the best solution, but a local perspective may only serve to complicate matters. When it comes to finding our way, there really is nothing better than a good map. Not only can a map tell us where we are, but it can also help us find where we want to go and how best to get there.

Having been led by the Holy Spirit to engage the people of a city with the gospel, one of the first things you need to do is survey and record the "lay of the land." This is best done through mapping—compiling a multi-layer graphical representation of the area in which you propose to be a missionary.

Mapping is an invaluable skill for all ministries. An outsider wanting to begin ministry in a new place can gain great value from walking the streets and documenting everything observed. People are greatly affected by the places in which they live, and by studying their environment one can learn much. As you study the city, you come to understand its people. This is the first step in incarnation—putting yourself in the shoes of those to whom you want to minister.

A map is the fieldwork out of which strategies can be formed. It's the gathering of intelligence that helps you plan your approach to ministry. It helps you organize your initial observations and coordinate with others to develop an understanding of how people think, live, and interact. It also serves as an introductory project—something to do in the community before you even know what to do in the community. It is a great way to initiate conversation, to become conversant in culture, and to effectively pray for your city.

A missionary map doesn't need to be drawn from scratch. Printed or online maps may be used. Your map may be drawn in a notebook, designed in Photoshop, or plotted on Google Maps. This working document will naturally change as the missionary gains insight. It will also need to be amended to show where God is obviously at work and there are opportunities for ministry. A map provides a bird's-eye view of the realities of the city that is helpful for training partners and for collaboration with other believers working in the same city. Sharing the information you've collected is as easy as passing on a copy of the map.

Of course, ministry requires more than just knowing the locations of streets and highways. To begin to truly understand the environment, observations must be made in multiple dimensions. Ideally, your map would have at least three layers: **geographic** (the layout of the city), **social** (where people live, work, and shop, how they behave and why), and **spiritual** (what people worship, revere, and fear).

## Geography: Mapping the Space

The first step in developing a map is to plot the physical locations in and around a city. In the 1960s American urban planner Kevin A. Lynch conducted an extensive study[1] of how urban-dwellers navigate their environments and outlined what he identified as the five "elements" of the city. These were the most basic building blocks of a person's understanding of the urban environment and have been used to great effect by missionaries and local church planters to help them understand the cities in which they find themselves.

### 1. Paths

The first element of a city is what Lynch referred to as "paths."[2] In mapping, paths are the streets, sidewalks, trails, and other channels along which people travel. These are usually delineated with lines on a map—thick for major thoroughfares, thin or dashed for minor routes. Urban paths may include pedestrian walkways, alleys, bus routes, or subway and metro lines. Many modern cities were built on rivers and railways, which are also paths.

Paths are important because they limit an individual's experience of the city and shape his perspective of it. If you want to relate to someone, follow his paths. For example, someone who gets around by subway may not be familiar with what's above him on his underground journey. Consequently, he only knows the areas of town at either end of his commute; these are the areas that shape his understanding of the city and influence him the most.

This phenomenon is clearly seen in "tourist" areas of major cities around the world. Along tour bus routes, things are typically more expensive but can seem much more inviting. Traveling solely along these paths might lead you to believe that a city is quite expensive, or

---

1 Lynch, *The Image of the City.*

2 Ibid., 49.

that everyone speaks English. Simply taking an alternate route may provide you with a more accurate perspective on things.

It is also important to consider the mode of transportation along a particular path. The same streets navigated by private car will provide a very different experience than for those traveling by bicycle. Mode of transportation will likewise affect one's perception of distance along a path. A bus that stops every two blocks can make a street seem much longer than it actually is simply because it takes so long to traverse. For urban dwellers, distance is a relative concept.

Exploring different paths can help you become familiar with a city. Even if you minister in a city you're extremely familiar with—the town in which you grew up—traveling along less-familiar paths will open your eyes to the experiences and perspectives of your neighbors. This exploration is where mapping begins.

## 2. Nodes

Nodes are centers of activity, such as plazas, squares, metro stations, parks, business centers, or shopping malls. These places, according to Lynch, are "strategic spots in a city into which an observer can enter" and allow for interaction.[3] Nodes are found at intersections, which are anywhere paths converge.

When paths cross, different sorts of people intermingle. At any given time of day, the wealthy and poor alike may be found standing together on a subway platform or street corner—something that is much less likely to happen at other points along a path. Nodes are important for gaining cultural insight because they provide the opportunity to see how these different people interact (or avoid interaction) with one another. Nodes are the best vantage points for people-watching.

Billboards, signs, and newsstands are usually found in nodes. Because nodes tend to be busy places, they are prime real estate for the dissemination of information. Organizations distribute flyers and vendors advertise here for maximum visibility. Gossip, news, and social updates happen in and around nodes. Of course, social networking has had a great impact on the spread of information by essentially becoming an additional system of virtual nodes.

---

3 Ibid, 72.

As people move into nodes, their behavior may change. Rather than traveling along a path and its predictable patterns for traffic flow and behavioral norms, the observer is thrown into a chaotic intermingling of multiple paths and the people using them. Consequently, people often enter a node with their guard up and their bags clutched tightly. Nodes may be a great place to disseminate information, but all the noise likely means they are not the best place to try to engage someone in meaningful conversation.

New York City's Grand Central Terminal is the largest train station in the world[4] and perhaps the most familiar node in the world. Twenty-one million visitors visit the immense, neoclassical structure each year making it the sixth most visited tourist attraction in the world.[5] From 5:30 a.m. to 2:00 a.m., thousands of people flood the station's 44 platforms, waiting for commuter, long-distance, and subway trains.

The diversity is staggering. New Yorkers from every walk of life can be found at Grand Central. Homeless people stand beside millionaires. Catholic priests, Jewish rabbis, and Muslim imams stand on the same platforms as they wait for the trains that will take them to their houses of worship. Representatives of every tribe, tongue, and nation shuffle their feet across the terminal's marble tile floor. Every day, thousands of people share the same space with people they would otherwise never have anything to do with. This node is more than an intersection of the city; it's where the peoples of the world cross paths.

Grand Central has great media "reach." The gaze of the thousands of eyes that pass through the station each day is worth a lot of money. Consequently, advertising is everywhere. The halls are lined with billboards and posters. Pillars on the platform are wrapped in banners. Monitors throughout the terminal display commercials that were specially produced for the fast-moving commuter audience. There is an Apple store in the terminal's main concourse. Religious groups distribute tracts; local businesses dispense flyers. Whatever you're trying to communicate, the Grand Central node is the place to get the word out.

The people passing through the terminal carry themselves a bit differently than they might in another setting. As if the invasion of personal space and bombardment of information weren't enough,

---

4 Wikimedia Foundation, Inc., "Grand Central Terminal."

5 Appleton et al., "World's Most-Visited Tourist Attractions."

commuters also have to be wary of pickpockets while they navigate the maze of trains and tunnels. They hold their belongings tighter, walk a bit quicker, and stare at the floor. Many people listen to their headphones, read a newspaper, or chat on their phones to drown out all the noise.

Not every node is as large or obvious as Grand Central. But the effects are still the same: the convergence of a diversity of people, the opportunity to distribute information to a broad audience, and a guarded posture for all who enter.

## 3. Districts

Districts are areas of a city with "perceived internal sameness."[6] This may be a neighborhood or group of neighborhoods that have a distinct character. Districts may be known for their past or present function (a "garment district," "stockyards"), their settlers or inhabitants (Chinatown, Little Italy), the historical reputation and social stigma (Skid Row, Hell's Kitchen, Red Light), architecture (historic, warehouse, tract housing additions), or geographic location (downtown, uptown, docks, waterfront, etc.).

Most urban dwellers develop a sense of identity around the districts in which they live, play, or do business. Each district has a reputation within the city, and brings the expectation that a certain "type" of person might be found there.

Districts play a key part in the development of a city's personality, and are determining factors in social segmentation. The district in which a person lives shapes a city-dweller's understanding of himself in relation to other members of society. This is evident in so-called "blue-collar" or "working-class" neighborhoods where social and economic forces can make it hard for someone to move away.

Neighborhoods are social groupings as well as geographic ones. For this reason, districts can be quite complex. Observe, for example, Bel Air, the West Los Angeles neighborhood of the rich and famous. Perfectly manicured landscaping lines the streets that wind through the gated properties dotted with mansions, pools, garages, and guesthouses. Even a complete outsider would recognize this as an affluent area.

A passing observation, however, does little to shed light on the makeup of Bel Air's community. During the day, the place is bustling

---

6 *The Image of the City*, 66.

with outsiders. Tourists snapping photos from double-decker tour buses. The gardeners, the pool boys, and the handymen—many of whom belong to ethnic minorities—could not afford to live in this neighborhood. At the local parks and playgrounds, nannies (usually immigrants) care for the children who live here. It isn't until evening that Bel Air's residents are home, and even then they tend to remain in the privacy of their own expensive homes.

Every population segment has its own subculture, language, and rules that present barriers and bridges to the spread of the gospel. When it comes to mission in the city, urban segmentation may be seen as analogous to the anthropological concept of "people groups," as outlined by missiologist Ralph Winter.[7] From this perspective, the missionary may need to take a different approach to gospel ministry for each district in the city.

## 4. Edges

Edges are the boundaries of a district. According to Lynch,[8] the linear elements not used or considered as paths by the observer are where one district ends and another may begin. Edges are the borders between two places, linear breaks in the continuity of the space. Common edges are things like shores, edges of a housing development, walls, highways, rivers, etc.

As a city grows, the construction of a new interstate or commercial zone might divide an older neighborhood, effectively making one district into two. In a district with heavy foot traffic, anything that is difficult to cross often forms an edge.

Leaving one district and entering another may be as simple as crossing a street. In other instances, tunnels, bridges, gates, and crossings allow people to move between districts. Other "edges" may be less obvious; we may not be able to pinpoint exactly where one district ends and another begins, but we know when we've moved from one to another.

In the United States, many cities were built alongside railroad tracks. These tracks were regarded as edges, and continue to have social implications in modern times. Oftentimes, certain minority groups would be relegated to living outside the city. This is where the term

---

7 Winter, "Unreached Peoples and Beyond (1974 to Now)."

8 *The Image of the City,* 62.

"from the other side of the tracks" came from, and it means "undesirable." As cities have grown around them, these sections of the city are now found in central "downtown" sections often considered "slums" or "ghettos." Edges such as these mean that physical proximity does not necessarily indicate similarity. Three people may live very close to one another in a city, but have very different experiences of that city.

Take, for example, the middle-class businessman. He has a nice family and lives in a nice house in a quiet neighborhood just outside, but not too far outside, the city center. Every day before work, the man takes his dog for a walk along streets called things like "Stone Creek Drive" and "Sunny Brook Lane." After breakfast with his wife and children, the man hops in his luxury sedan and drives in to work, parks in his company's private parking garage, and takes the elevator up to his office on the 18th floor where he enjoys a sweeping view of the city he loves.

Next, consider the third-generation shopkeeper. She lives in an apartment across town from the bookshop her grandfather opened years ago. Her days are long, beginning at 6:00 a.m., when she climbs out of bed and dashes to catch her train to work. For thirty-seven minutes, she's hurtled through an underground tunnel, oblivious of what's happening above her at the street level. After arriving at her stop, she passes through the rough neighborhood that was once the city's center of commerce. She buys a cup of coffee from the food cart on the corner and arrives just in time to unlock the door and turn the sign over from "closed" to "open." All day long, the shopkeeper watches the city she loves from the windows of the bookshop.

Now, imagine the daily routine of an immigrant. Relatively new to the city, he hasn't yet found a job or a place of his own. Since he's sleeping on his cousin's sofa, he gets up early and helps around the house. Every day he goes to the government offices where he's been trying to apply for permission to stay in the country. After that the man hits the streets looking for a job. Without a residence permit or a permanent address, there's not a lot of work. Because he doesn't speak the language very well, every interaction is difficult. He misses his wife and children back home, but he's here to make a better life for them. These days aren't easy, but the man is thankful to be in the city he sees in the reflection of the windows he passes as he searches for a "help wanted" sign.

The three people outlined above are all neighbors, in the sense that they may live quite near to one another. In fact, they may cross paths every day. But the edges that separate these individuals give them very different experiences of the city. The businessman loves the city, but he almost always experiences it through the glass of very protected routes and comfortable vantage points. The districts at either end of his drive to and from work are filled with the same sorts of people. The shopkeeper, on the other hand, puts on earphones and holds tightly to her purse during her commute because on the subway people who are very different from her press in on her on all sides. The immigrant doesn't yet know how to "read" this place and can't yet tell whether people are happy to see him, hostile toward him, or indifferent. Until he can begin to understand, the city is a hostile place with no room for him.

Distance is also skewed according to the edges each person crosses. The businessman lives much farther away from his office than the shopkeeper lives from her bookshop, but her commute via public transportation takes twice as long as his on the expressway. For the immigrant, the city is enormous, far larger than the twenty square blocks he covers on foot each day on his job-hunting rounds. He knows one district and has yet to cross any edges at all.

The missionary must pay particular attention to the edges. All too often, the missionary thinks in terms of physical proximity and access while ignoring the social boundaries that have been set up all around the city.

Crossing boundaries isn't the job of the residents; it's the job of the missionary. Of course, as people come to faith and are discipled toward maturity, they should be challenged to move beyond the edges, to deliberately leave one district in order to live out the gospel in another. Inviting people to cross an edge in order to hear the gospel may get in the way of inviting them to follow Jesus.

## 5. Landmarks

The word "landmarks" brings to mind towers and monuments, but when mapping, anything that stands out as noticeable can serve as a landmark. Lynch found that people use such objects, structures, and places to navigate the city.[9] In giving directions to outsiders, residents use easily recognized landmarks: "Turn right at the drug store." For

---

9 Ibid., 78.

insiders, they may use something more familiar, like "turn at Kevin's house."

Barcelona lies at the foot of a mountain on the Mediterranean Sea. Spain's second-largest urban center is laid out in a grid of straight streets and square city blocks. But the orientation of these streets is not "north-south" but rather "northeast-southwest," so citizens instead refer to "upper" and "lower" sections of town. In Barcelona's case, the mountain and the sea are landmarks that allow people to orient themselves.

Landmarks can be architectural details, such as distinctive gas-lit street lamps, cobblestone streets, or white picket fences—anything that helps a person determine where he is. Even if the landmarks don't give away exact locations, an insider can use them to decipher what sort of place she's in. In many cities, immigrant neighborhoods are marked with satellite dishes (to get broadcasts from home) and clothes drying on clotheslines (clothes dryers can be expensive).

Landmarks usually have lasting historical and cultural significance as well. A city built on a river will be shaped by it in many ways. Portland, Oregon, was built on the Willamette and Columbia rivers. As an inland port in the mid 1800s, it was a temporary home for sailors from all over the world who had money to spend. Consequently, the city's first economy was built on alcohol and sex. To this day, Portland (or Pornland, as locals have been known to call it) is home to more strip clubs per capita (7.4 for every 100,000 residents) than any other city in the U.S.[10] The ubiquity of these establishments has done much to normalize the sex trade there. According to a recent report,[11] it has also been linked to higher rates of human trafficking and sexual abuse. To this day, the rivers are a subconscious reminder of the city's history of vice and exploitation.

In Riga, Latvia, the Freedom Monument stood as a symbol of national independence amidst Soviet occupation. The Chiang Kai-shek Memorial Hall in Taipei stands as a constant reminder of the conservative Chinese leader's ouster from the mainland and exile to the island of Taiwan. "Christ the Redeemer," the 130-foot-tall concrete and soapstone statue of Jesus overlooking Rio de Janeiro, was built by private donations just after Brazil became a secular republic. These landmarks have significant and lasting effects on the people who pass

---

10 Brunner, ""When it comes to strip Clubs, Portland has nothing to hide."

11 Hannah-Jones, "Human trafficking industry thrives in Portland metro area."

them every day. Symbols of rebellion, oppression, religion, and independence emblazon themselves on the hearts of the citizens of a city.

In His earthly ministry, Jesus used landmarks to His advantage. In John 4, we read that Jesus found the "woman at the well" at Jacob's Well in Samaria. This landmark would have been a central part of life for many Samaritans, but different types of people would have been found there at different times of the day. His "Sermon on the Mount" used that landmark to both facilitate and distinguish what would become His best-known teachings. The same would have been true of various city gates, mountains, the rivers, and so on.

In fact, God's people are instructed to be builders of landmarks. In the book of Joshua reside eight examples of the Israelites piling rocks at the sites of His special provision, protection, or victory. These monuments served as reminders to future generations of God's faithfulness. In many cases, it can be said that a city's existing monuments, though built in ignorance of God's role, might also be redeemed with memories of the Most High. The missionary can use landmarks as bridges for the communication of the gospel.

## High Places

Thom Wolf, who was among the first sociologists to apply Lynch's findings to urban missions, has pointed out[12] that each layer of the map informs the others. For example, in most cultures, areas with higher physical elevations tend to be assigned some level of importance. "Sacred" structures are often built in these locations and can have significant influence upon a city's history and culture. High places, therefore, can have direct spiritual significance to a missionary's work.

Athens, like most Roman cities, was an acropolis built on a hilltop to make it visible yet easily defended. The most important buildings—temples, palaces, castles, and government buildings—were built on the highest points. In Acts 17, we read that the Apostle Paul went up to the Areopagus, an amphitheater-like structure built on a hilltop, where philosophers and city elders would gather to discuss current events, consider social issues, and make decisions. This "high place" had spiritual significance to the missionary and provided a tremendous opportunity for contextualized gospel proclamation.

---

12 Wolf, "The City."

In nearly every city in the world, the high places are significant historically, culturally, geographically, and spiritually. The very existence of high places says much about the people who built them. By observing the high places, you'll see how people in your city assign value and meaning to places. They don't treat all people and places equally. Power, importance, and influence are either ascribed, earned, or bought, and whatever the city's fathers have done in raised elevations will reveal what influences the citizens of that city. High places should be among the first things plotted on the missionary's map.

## Social: Mapping the Story

After plotting the geography of the city, the missionary should begin the social layer of the map. This layer includes who lives where, what they do, what their needs are, and how they see themselves in relation to the rest of the city. The purpose of this layer of the map is to help the missionary understand the people to whom he has been sent. This information can only come through personal interaction. As one may imagine, this section of the map may contain sensitive information such as prayer requests, needs, or personal struggles. It may be strange for a friend from your neighborhood to enter your house only to find his name written on a map displayed on your wall. Please use discretion.

**Demographics**, information about the people who live in a place, are fairly easy to discover. For starters, there are various sources of demographic research findings from books to newspapers to online resources. Take demographic research with a grain of salt. Some of these studies tend to be completed under social and political pressures, and their findings can sometimes be skewed. For example, a local government may have an interest in finding a higher number of people living in poverty within the city because that could mean greater funding from the state. Other problematic statistics, such as crime rates, education scores, and recipients of social services, may likewise be downplayed or exaggerated to serve an ideological agenda.

Beginning with an intentional observation on the street, the missionary can quickly get a sense of who lives where. But demographics run deeper than what can be seen on the surface. Not all outsiders look as though they don't belong. Some immigrant groups can be harder to find because they do a better job of integrating into their host cultures. Likewise, not everyone who seems out of place truly is. An accurate map requires personal interaction.

One strategy for demography involves survey work. Missionaries often send volunteers out into the nodes of a city to ask people anonymous questions about themselves. "How many people live with you?" may give an indication of a residential district's population. Questions like "What is this area known for?" or "What sorts of people live in this neighborhood?" can be extremely helpful because they provide more than cold, hard facts. These questions allow respondents to give their perception of the reality, which for the purposes of social mapping, can be much more valuable.

Another way to compile the same information is to find reliable cultural informants. These insiders, usually unaware of their role in mapping, will be able to provide the missionary with a good understanding of a people from their own perspective. Ask a cultural informant where to find Algerian immigrants in the city, and he may not be able to specifically identify that group. But ask him where foreigners tend to hang out, and it will be likely that he knows various hangouts frequented by outsiders.

**Need** may be more difficult to gauge. Not everyone will be open and honest about his needs, especially with a stranger. Common needs would include physical security, financial stability, or companionship. Believe it or not, many people who live in large cities suffer a severe sense of loneliness. Experiencing these needs is one thing but confessing them might be another. Few people are willing to confess those needs that might make them appear weak. In order for the map to accurately reflect the needs of the community, the missionary must do a bit of investigating.

Although needs are generally individual, there is great value to annotating need on a map. What may initially seem to be an isolated incident of need may, in fact, be a community-wide problem. Mapping will help to reveal societal needs at the neighborhood and district levels. This insight can be particularly helpful in the development of strategies for community service.

**Narrative** is the story a community believes about itself. This story (or set of stories) is perhaps the most helpful part of the missionary's map.

Sometimes, narrative is not a conscious thing. For example, someone who lives in a working-class neighborhood may use derogatory descriptions of the wealthy who live nearby but be unaware of his prejudice against them. Another may naturally refer to himself deprecatingly, a sign of low social status.

The message of Christ is for all people everywhere. Narrative mapping allows the missionary to discern exactly how the gospel is good news to a particular group of people. Those with a victim mentality would be overjoyed to know that Christ brings justice and frees the oppressed (Luke 4:18). Those who find themselves caught in the trap of materialism need to know that the things of this world will one day pass away (1 John 2:17). Idol worshipers need to know the futility of their misguided affections (Jeremiah 10:1–5).

Through direct conversations we can begin to truly know our neighbors. We can patch together a rough outline of how people see the world around them: their personal religious experience, their goals for life, and their dreams for the future. Ultimately, this is how we can know the best way to communicate the fact that only Jesus can supply what people everywhere are looking for.

As with need, narrative may at first seem to be unrelated to geography. But mapping narrative can bring into focus neighborhood histories that are highly influential for the neighbors who live there. Adding this dimension to your map can help you see how local events can have lasting effects on the people who live in a particular area, regardless of whether those people were actually present when those events occurred.

### Spiritual: Mapping God's Activity

The final layer of the missionary's map, the spiritual layer, is the most important to the missionary's work. Long before the missionary is sent, God has been working among the people of the earth. He reveals Himself through nature, conscience, and blessing. He demonstrates His character through the presence of His people around the world. Through the Scriptures He makes Himself known as a personal God. He is not "served by human hands, as though He needed anything," yet His gospel is spread by means of humanity.

In his 1990 book, *Experiencing God*, Henry Blackaby famously wrote, "when God reveals to you where He is working, that becomes His invitation to join Him in His activity."[13] As missionaries, we begin engagement by discovering where God is at work. This isn't about voices

---

13 Blackaby, *Experiencing God*, 56.

from heaven or extra-biblical revelation; the missionary discovers God at work by prayerfully interjecting himself into the society to whom he is called.

Having a map that shows the physical layout of the city and the social narrative of its people, a missionary may now turn to marking those people, opportunities, events, and places he recognizes as being spiritually significant. Physical spaces can provide an indication of possible areas of spiritual significance. Social spaces, high places, and existing spiritual structures are often frontline areas. A community's stories can also be an indicator of God's activity. Conflict, failure, success, and art can point to spiritual movement. But ultimately, prayerful interaction with people is the best way to be led by God into what He's been doing.

# MAPPING: HOW-TO

## Mapping the Geography

Begin with the **geographical layer**. A street map is a good start or a printed map from Google. Some practitioners prefer to draw the map by hand as it allows them to include the distortions caused by modes of travel, hard edges, or other features that may not be clear on a regular map. If you prefer to keep the project electronic, Google Maps is a great place to start. Just be sure that your base layer shows the entirety of your focus: a region, city, neighborhood, district, or other section of the city.

Whatever the format, your map must be accessible. You should be able to easily make additions and annotations to the map as observations are made. For this reason, you may choose to carry a companion notebook, iPad, smartphone, or some other way to jot down notes to be included in the project.

Perhaps the simplest way to mark the elements of the city is to draw directly on the map using different color markers. Pushpins and colored string can be used when making holes in the wall isn't a concern. Another possible approach is to use transparent sheets that can be removed as not to obscure other information on the map such as street names and neighborhood names.

Your map is only as good as the information it shows, so be sure it includes any locations that may be significant to society, such as centers of government, education, and commerce. Many locations in urban environments are dual- or multi-use, so be creative in how you show the changing importance of various locations. Also, some annotations on your map, such as farmers' markets, festivals, and celebrations may be time-dependent. Layering labels and details can help you show these realities on the map.

Keep in mind that the purpose of this layer is to help you see the city through the eyes of the locals. To this end, it may be a good idea to color-code your map to draw connections. For example, if members of a certain population segment are primarily found in three different districts and tend to frequent eight different paths, you can show that connection by indicating those with the same color.

Map out more than one way to get to any given point, and be sure to keep a key for your map. This will facilitate the sharing of all the information gathered and will help with the identification of the various elements at a glance. Kevin Lynch proposed annotating a map using these symbols:

PATHS      NODES      DISTRICTS      EDGES      LANDMARKS

## Mapping the Social Layer

The next layer of the map will reflect **social** observations of your city. This layer will indicate who lives where and the cursory information that can be found about them. In essence, this will show stereotypes and generalizations about the people who live in each sector of the map. Mark these things by using notes, labels, and note cards.

A good way to map the narrative of a district is to include clippings from local newspapers and magazines. An article about crime in a neighborhood, for example, would be relevant. Printed statistics for local schools would be particularly helpful in painting a picture of the condition of local education. The same would be true of information about businesses and profiles of residents.

The social layer would also be the place to mark information about new friends and contacts made. The name of a helpful realtor or the office of an especially sympathetic government official would help the missionary understand the social landscape of the city. This is the place to collect addresses, phone numbers, and any other information that might help in making connections. Including photographs of new people and places is a great way to remember names.

Consider the narrative layer of the map as a composite profile. The personal stories, examples of need, and news articles all fit together like puzzle pieces depicting a collage of a community's story. Each observation may not apply to the entire city or population segment but its presence nevertheless affects the story of the whole.

## Mapping the Spiritual Layer

The third layer of the map shows the spiritual realities of the city. This section will include churches, temples, idols, evidence of the occult, or any other place you consider to be of significance.

Think of the spiritual layer as a prayer guide. By using the spiritual information contained in this layer of the map, insightful intercession may be made by volunteers through prayer. It can even help people who have not even visited a city pray for it by outlining specific needs and opportunities.

Another great use for this spiritual layer is to record place and frequency of spiritual conversation. For example, you make weekly visits to a local farmers' market and have profound personal conversations about Christ nearly every visit. If, after each encounter, you were to mark that encounter on the map, it would quickly become clear that the market is a spiritually significant place. When it comes time to make decisions about where to send volunteers, place team members, or start a Bible study, the map would reveal the strategic importance of the farmers' market.

Finally, be sure the completed map can be easily shared with others. As God blesses any missionary team with new members, the map is a great way to quickly bring them up to speed on what cultural insight the team has been able to gather. The map should be readily shared with the sending churches and other supporters of the work. As local people come to faith, it would be particularly interesting to consult them regarding the information collected on the map to see how the observations of an outsider compare with those of an insider.

# EXEGETING CULTURE

## [chapter 4]

BY CALEB CRIDER

One of the most well-known stories in human history is that of the Great Flood. Who could forget? The tale of watery judgment upon a wicked generation. Mercy extended to one righteous man and his family. The man's obedience in the face of ridicule and uncertainty. The waters covering the face of the earth. Hope in the face of utter destruction. Joy at the sight of a dove with a green branch. It's a timeless story, a cautionary tale of mankind's place in the universe. Here's the story, as millions of people know it:

> The fish instructed Manu to build a large ship, as the flood now only months away. As the rains began, Manu tied a rope from his ship to the ghasha, which safely guided him as the waters rose. The waters grew so high that the entire earth was covered. As the waters subsided, the ghasha guided Manu to a mountaintop.[1]

Does this sound familiar? This flood story is present in Hindu folklore that predates Christianity on the Indian subcontinent. An anthropologist will tell you that cultures around the world tell remarkably similar stories—creation myths, flood stories, and tales of brothers killing brothers. Every culture has elements of the human story, fragments, perspectives, human-sided versions of what really happened. This is no accident; it is God's provision for reintroducing Himself to those who have turned away from Him. Paul refers to this pattern in his letter to the Roman Church:

> For what can be known about God is plain to them, because God has shown it to them. For his invisible attributes, namely, his eternal power and divine nature, have been clearly perceived, ever since the creation of the world, in the things that have been made. So they are without excuse. For although they knew God, they did not honor him as God or give thanks to him, but they became futile in their thinking, and their foolish hearts were darkened. Claiming to be wise, they became fools, and exchanged the glory of the immortal God for images resembling mortal man and birds and animals and creeping things.[2]

---

1 Bierlein, *Parallel Myths*, 125.

2 Romans 1:19–23.

Paul begins the book of Romans with a cosmic perspective on humanity's relationship to God. Humanity, if we may speak of it as a whole, once knew God; Adam and Eve walked with Him in the garden in perfect community with their Creator. But then sin entered the picture and has diverted mankind's worship away from the Most High. Having "exchanged the truth about God for lies," humanity worshiped and served the created things rather than the Creator."

This is the beginning of the story for every people in every culture —rebellion. Sin is blinding, and most societies have suppressed the memory of where they came from. Instead, people create their own origin stories, deny their God-given purpose, and thereby explain away their own existence. Every culture shares in common a similar memory of the themes of the human story: *We were once at peace with our Creator, but then we rebelled. Since then, we have struggled to regain fellowship with Him.* This reframing of reality is universal. You can see it in any culture as you listen to its stories, study its religions, and investigate its worldview.

But God is faithful. He has not left His creation without hope. In the "fullness of time," God sent Jesus.[3] With the Incarnation of the Son, God interrupted the pagan story of one particular culture in order to reveal Himself to all mankind. He tore down the false realities they had constructed, reminding them of their true origins as His creation made for community with Him.

## Culture

As the Author of history and the Creator of humankind, God values culture. Throughout the story of humanity, from beginning to end, God creates and preserves human diversity. In Genesis 11, we read that the people of the earth had become united in their pride and built a tower as a monument to their own glory. God intervened by separating the people and confusing their language so that they could not communicate. In essence, God fights human rebellion with diversity. In this He demonstrates that He is glorified through the creation and existence of various cultures.

In the Book of Revelation, John sees a vision of people from every "tribe, tongue, and nation" gathered in worship around God's throne.[4]

---

3 Galatians 4:4.

4 Revelation 7:9.

To John, what is so striking about this vision is that although the great multitude is unified in their worship, the group is still somehow diverse enough that he notices the differences among them. The picture here is not only of ethnic diversity, but of social diversity. In this Revelation, God reveals that He desires to be worshiped by different types of people. He is powerful enough to divide us and then to unite us to His glory.

Human diversity also has great value to the Church. Experience across cultures allows us to see how God is worshiped by people who are different from us. Christians around the world sing to God, but we sing very different songs with remarkably different tunes. God's people in different places have unique expressions of worship: some dance, others fall to their faces. Some pray aloud, others meditate in silence. The Revelation shows us that God is pleased with this creative diversity, and promises His presence among His people as they worship. And while God's people are those who lift up His name, it isn't only the believers among the nations of the earth who remember Him.

Observe any culture in depth, and it becomes clear that the suppressed memory of the Creator is not completely forgotten. Man is continuously confronted with the revelation of God's attributes through nature.[5] Furthermore, tribes around the world — from ethnolinguistic people groups like the Criollos of Peru or the Jhora of India, to urban subcultures such as Brooklyn hipsters, or third-generation Chinese immigrants in San Francisco — all have been left with the faintest notion that God exists and that things have gone terribly wrong among us.

When you're really looking for this narrative, you can find it woven into every aspect of culture. Musicians who have only experienced human love sing about its power. Storytellers focus on themes of redemption. Unjust people, who do only "what is right in their own eyes," continue to wrestle for justice. Advertisements promise their products will provide fulfillment. Religion demonstrates man's best efforts to earn righteousness. Everywhere you look, threads lead back to God. The Artist has left His fingerprints on His work.

"For his invisible attributes, namely, his eternal power and divine nature, have been clearly *perceived*, ever since the creation of the world, in the things that have been made."[6] These invisible attributes have

---

5 Romans 1:19.

6 Romans 1:20.

70

great potential for our missionary efforts. Like every good story with a twist in its plot, it all makes sense in hindsight. God's purposes, His presence, His faithful provision are much easier to see in light of salvation. Rather than having to introduce a foreign truth, missionaries take the opportunity to retell a people's stories back to them from the Kingdom perspective.

In the Scriptures, cultural exegesis is referred to as "perception."[7] The word, translated from the ancient Greek word "to understand," meant "insight based on observation."

Paul employed this very technique when he "perceived" that the citizens of Athens were devoutly religious (Acts 17:22–33). He observed shrines, monuments, and temples to various gods, recognizing that even the Greek pantheon of god-myths left people longing for more. Their vague memory of humanity's connection to the Creator had led them to develop a dramatic mythology of gods behind everything they couldn't explain. Just to be sure they hadn't missed a god, they had erected at least one monument in honor of "the unknown god."

Paul took advantage of this bridge into the culture. Rather than begin the conversation by confronting their blatant idolatry, Paul told the Athenians that he knew this God they were afraid of overlooking. The Greek worldview had room for an unknown god. Paul knew the God these people had "forgotten." He proclaimed the gospel by telling the men of Athens their own story back to them in light of the gospel.

Just as cultures have bridges that facilitate the spread of the gospel, they also have barriers to it. The rituals and superstitions that people revere in place of God often keep them from understanding Him. Recognizing these barriers can likewise inform our missionary strategies. Successful communication of the gospel requires that we navigate meanings, misperceptions, and deeply held ideologies.

I recently found myself in a deep spiritual conversation with a neighbor. He is spiritually agnostic, and doesn't believe that humans can know God, or even whether He exists. He remembers going to church a few times as a child, but he otherwise has no religious background. We spoke about the role of religion in society, and I tried to move the conversation from ritual and tradition to a personal relationship with Christ. You can imagine my surprise when he declared, "We Christians are responsible for committing many atrocities in the name of God."

---

7 Ancient Greek, γινωσκω (ginosko). Gowan, *The Westminster Theological Wordbook of the Bible*, 280.

"*We? Christians?* I thought you weren't religious," I said, "maybe I misunderstood you?"

"Oh, I'm not," my neighbor explained, "but I'm more Christian than Muslim."

To my neighbor, "Christian" wasn't a spiritual state or even a category of belief. It was a cultural label synonymous with concepts of Western, Enlightenment, American, and rational. My neighbor certainly understood there was a difference between my version of Christianity and his, but from his perspective I was the one co-opting the term from common American culture. According to him, we're all Christians. In the United States, a major barrier to the spread of the gospel is the predominance of cultural Christianity. It's difficult to declare the good news to people who greatly misunderstand it.

Other cultures have different barriers to the spread of the gospel. Societal prejudices, traditions, and ethnic tensions often prevent broad sowing of the good news. Some cultures lack even a basic spiritual vocabulary that allows for the meaningful communication of abstract concepts like God and Spirit. Imagine trying to teach someone about prayer, worship, heaven, or sin when they don't have words for any of those things!

Despite the barriers a culture may present, we are called to communicate the transforming message of salvation in Christ alone. This requires we study culture in search of bridges that facilitate the spread of the gospel and the barriers that need to be overcome in order for disciples to be made. We refer to this process of intentional, hands-on research as cultural exegesis.

## Exegesis of a Culture

The word *exegesis* literally means "to draw out" and is applied to the act of studying something (text, art, language) and extracting meaning from it. The opposite is *eisegesis* (literally "to draw in"), where the observer interprets his findings through his own presuppositions.

Sound theology requires exegesis of Scripture. In order to avoid creating God in our own image, we must glean our understanding of who God is by studying His Word and taking meaning from it. In the same way, sound missiology requires exegesis of culture. Contextual immersion allows us to identify with our audiences and communicate effectively with them. It is much easier to love people who you know and understand.

Unfortunately, exegeting culture can be difficult and time-consuming. Objectivity is impossible, so our tendency is to interpret what we observe in others through the lens of our own presuppositions. When we see something in one culture that brings to mind an evil common in our own culture, it's difficult not to assign that same meaning to the culture we're attempting to study.

In southern Spain, the annual Candlemas celebration features men who wear white, cone-shaped hoods and white robes as they march through the streets carrying large wooden crosses. A missionary from the southern United States would surely need to fight against associating this with the white supremacist group Ku Klux Klan, who wear the same garb. In many eastern cultures, silence is a sign of respect, and eye contact is rude. In many western cultures, the opposite is true: Anyone who doesn't speak up and look someone directly in the eye isn't to be trusted. In ancient India, the symbol of the swastika represents wishes of future success. In the parts of the world touched by World War II, it's the symbol of Nazism.

Different cultures assign different meanings to various symbols, beliefs, and behaviors. This is called cultural relativism. The only way to learn these different meanings is to become a student of those cultures. This requires deliberately and prayerfully exposing yourself to those things that influence and shape the culture you've decided to study.

Cultural exegesis is a basic missionary skill that allows us to see a people's context through spiritual eyes that discern the bridges and barriers to the communication of the gospel. Because culture is dynamic and multifaceted, it can be difficult to even know where to begin. I recommend you begin exegeting four key dimensions: story, space, idols, and conflict. While this list is not comprehensive, these four areas are common to nearly all cultures and all places, and provide a great deal of insight into a culture's bridges and barriers to the gospel.

## Story

I was watching Paul Giamatti play the lead role in the Tom Hanks-produced HBO miniseries, *John Adams*, when it occurred to me that nearly everything I know about history, I learned by watching Hollywood movies. I didn't even know about the Apollo 13 thing until, well, *Apollo 13*. *Forrest Gump* taught me about three presidents, Elvis Presley, and the Black Panthers. *Saving Private Ryan* exposed me to the horrors of World War II. *Charlie Wilson's War* showed me the backstory of America's involvement in Afghanistan. Come to think of it, Tom Hanks taught me all the history I know.

It's quite embarrassing to admit that my understanding of history depends on box-office success, but I suspect I'm not alone. For my entire life, my public school history lessons had to compete with movie stars and special effects. Unfortunately, the medium has a tendency to oversimplify.

This is why we tend to think in terms of "good guys versus bad guys" or "rags to riches" — it's how the stories are told to us. British literary critic Christopher Booker declared in 2005 there are only seven basic story plots in the world,[8] and my Hollywood education in history reflects that.

Story is central to community. Every culture maintains a collective memory through its folk tales, hero stories, tropes, and jokes. These stories are how we establish our identities, transmit our values, and pass down our histories.

Author Donald Miller says that truth is conveyed through story, not through rational systems.[9] Heavily influenced by creative writing professor and screenwriter Robert McKee, Miller encourages Christians to see the truth that is played out in the real lives of regular people. In his textbook on screenwriting, McKee asserts that narrative is basic and essential to all cultures everywhere. "Story," he writes, "is the currency of human contact."[10] Miller, who now hosts an annual "Storyline Conference" in Portland, builds on this concept, applying it to the lives of Christians on mission by teaching them the importance of story and seeking to inspire them to "tell a better one."[11]

Every community has a story. The sort of overarching story shaping a culture may not be emblazoned on a plaque in the center of town, but it's no less central to that culture. Its presence is likely more subtle. It can be found in the cautionary tales told by grandparents to their grandchildren. It can be found in the films, books, and viral memes that resonate with members of a tribe. The story may not have a title and probably isn't bound in a book, but members of a culture know the story by heart. It's in the collective consciousness of every member of a group.

---

8 Booker, *The Seven Basic Plots*, 4.

9 Dodd, "A Better Storyteller."

10 McKee, *Story*, 27.

11 Miller, *A Million Miles in a Thousand Years*, 66.

Andrew Jones, missionary, blogger, and global nontraditional church guru, has often said that his job is to "throw parties and tell stories." Thom Wolf taught that the missionary's role is to retell people's stories back to them in light of the gospel. This is very good missionary tradecraft indeed: find out what people are talking about, and show them how it all relates back to the Most High God.

Jesus was the master of retelling people's stories back to them. To a group of Pharisees, He told the story of a Pharisee who was proud and certain of his righteousness and a tax collector who was full of regret and self-loathing.[12] The Pharisees were familiar with the story they thought Jesus was telling. It was the one they had been writing for generations: They, the truly devoted and holy, distanced themselves from sin by following strict rules and by condemning everyone around them, especially sinners and tax collectors. But Jesus wasn't telling the story in the same way the Pharisees had. He added a twist at the end that showed the spiritual reality. In this parable, it is the tax collector, not the Pharisee, who is justified. The tax collector gets it right because he acknowledges his own unworthiness and need. Jesus flips the story upside-down in order to show the kingdom.

This is good cultural exegesis. Jesus didn't introduce a new story; He retold a familiar one. His audience heard themselves in the story, and realized the story was about them. Even those among them who were neither Pharisees nor tax collectors knew full well what Jesus meant — it's not the outward appearances of religion that God is concerned with; it's our inner contrition and repentance.

## Space

Another area for exegesis is the organization, maintenance, and use of space. Levels of trust, social structure, economic systems, and political ideologies can all be discerned through the observation of a people's living arrangements.

Remember: Meaning is drawn out through observation. The distance between houses, for example, can reveal much about a community, but the reasons a group might share close quarters may not be obvious. Villagers in the mountains of Yemen tend to huddle their homes close together for protection from the elements. The townships of shacks and huts surrounding Zimbabwe's cities are densely packed

---

12 Luke 18:9–14.

because prior to independence in 1980, black people wanted to live as close to the city as possible but were prohibited from living too close to town. New Yorkers live close together because the city was established to facilitate commerce and share resources. Exegesis of neighborhoods, villages, and cities can demonstrate a great deal about people if you look beyond what can be seen on the surface.

The key to understanding how people relate to their environment is finding evidence of change. While giving a tour through Los Angeles' Skid Row, sociologist Michael Mata pointed to streets of 1930s-era houses to illustrate the subtle signs of change.[13] On one of the streets, the houses are all roughly the same size and age, but range in condition from immaculate to dilapidated. Yard work, it turns out, is a great indicator of urban change.

Upkeep gives us insight into the demographics of a neighborhood. Young families may have lawns littered with toys. College kids may have lawns littered with beer cans. As people retire from their full-time jobs, Mata says, they have a lot more time to mow their lawns and plant flowers, and tend to care about those things. But as they age, homeowners increasingly can't keep up the yard work. If they can't afford to pay a gardener, the property becomes neglected. Rundown appearances may mean older residents.

Another sign of an aging demographic is visible security. Seniors may have been around through many changes on the block and are likely to have seen several rises and falls in crime, property values, and gentrification. The elderly who are sometimes alone for the first time in their lives often don't feel safe in their own homes. They compensate by installing deadbolts, alarm systems, and bars on the windows and doors. If you notice steel-grate screen doors, it's likely an older person's home.

Residents who own their homes have reason to care for their homes. After all, homeownership is an investment, and property values depend on things like landscaping and curb appeal. Renters, on the other hand, don't have as much incentive to care for things. Mowing the lawn and trimming the hedges is a lot of effort just to maintain someone else's investment. If the leaves are raked and the walkways are swept, it's likely the residents are homeowners.

Being a renter or a homeowner influences a person beyond his investment portfolio. It affects his state of mind. Ownership is a symbol

---

13 Michael Mata is the Director of Urban Development for World Vision. Michael Mata, presented at Origins Conference, Los Angeles, California, July 23, 2010.

of identification and settlement; these residents have literally bought into the neighborhood. Neighborhoods with higher levels of homeownership tend to be more connected, involved, and secure. We experienced the difference between renting and owning firsthand when we bought the house where we currently live.

We were still living in Barcelona when we decided to move to Portland, Oregon. We didn't know the city well at all, but through the online classifieds site craigslist.com, we found a house to rent on the north side of town. We'd never had a backyard before, or a garage. After several years in tiny Spanish apartments, the little brown 1930s Cape Cod seemed huge to us. As we moved in, our neighbors watched through their window blinds.

We made an effort to get to know our new neighbors but that proved difficult. The only time Dolores, the 98-year-old widow who lived next door, would speak to us was to complain when someone parked in front of her house. The retired couple across the street would wave hello but weren't interested in chatting. Peter, who lived down the street, refused the cookies we made him for Christmas on account of not knowing us well enough to eat anything we had made. Nevertheless, we grew fond of our little neighborhood.

As our one-year rental contract was coming to an end, we asked our landlord about buying the house. But the landlord was making too much money from the property to consider selling. When the young couple who lived next door needed to move for work, we ended up buying their little blue house, which was just like the one we had been renting. That move was the easiest ever—18 feet north, into a house with an identical floor plan.

Our life continued much as it had for the previous year, but we noticed a change in the way our neighbors interacted with us. Dolores would shout hello through the bars on her doorway every time we walked by. The retired couple became the friendliest people in the world, giving us furniture and offering the use of their tools. Peter would stop by to complain about fuzzy property lines and unjust zoning laws. I believe he accepted our Christmas cookies that year.

As renters, neighbors had seen us as tourists passing through without putting down roots. They had seen families like ours come and go, and it wasn't worth investing in us emotionally. By buying a house, however, we were showing that we were here to stay. We were casting our lot with this group of people, and tying our fate to its prosperity. We had become one of them.

This made sense to us, as Christ had modeled similar behavior in His incarnation. When the Word became flesh[14], He "bought a home" (His body) in the human neighborhood. In the past, God had spoken to humanity through prophets, but through the incarnation, He spoke through His Son.[15] This shift from speaking through messengers and dreams to speaking through a Son, was a deliberate act of a missionary God modeling what should be common missionary tradecraft.

Homeownership is a value for our neighborhood, but exegesis will reveal whether this is the case in your context. You may find that your neighbors are all renters, or that they see owning a home as participating in an unethical and materialistic system. The point is that you don't know how to best live out the gospel among a people until you've done your research.

Cultural exegesis of the space must extend well beyond just housing. Art and architecture, for example, play a big part in shaping how people understand and interact with their environment. Displays of art can both shape and reflect public sentiment by expressing ideas in tangible ways. Architecture can demonstrate how a community perceives its structures. Religious buildings may be very ornate in order to evoke the mystical. Government buildings might be utilitarian in design so as to indicate austerity and functionality. These details can tell much about the values and ideologies of those who designed, funded, and built the spaces.

Likewise, modes and patterns of transportation through and across the space can provide terrific insight into a group's attitudes and values. Public rail, bus, and ferry systems are usually run and subsidized by a government that also provides other basic services. An abundance of private taxis and buses might indicate that few people have personal transportation. Many cities swarm with bicycles because automobile traffic is so congested. A man riding a mule in a metropolitan city may originally be from a rural area. High-rise buildings with elevators could likely be newer and more expensive than their generally less expensive walkup counterparts.

Your observations only tell part of the story. The insight gained through what you see from the outside must be interpreted though the

---

14 John 1:14.

15 Hebrews 1:1–2.

eyes of an insider. You can observe how a community utilizes its space in different ways, but only time and experience can tell you why.

## Idols

"Man's nature," Calvin wrote in his *Institutes of the Christian Religion*, "is a perpetual factory of idols."[16] This is evident in the city. Typically, the word idol brings to mind "carved stones of primitive people."[17] But idolatry is much more than bronze statues perched in shrines to the mythological gods.

It's easy to spot the Buddhist shrine in the corner of a *dim sum* restaurant or the totem poles on the beaches of Hawaii, but idolatry isn't always so obvious. Human beings can put anything and everything in place of God in their lives. When you look at the city in this light, many more idols, often subtler, can be seen. Anything can be an idol, but some things have been made into what theologian Tim Keller has called "functional saviors"—those things that help even if temporarily to assuage our feelings of guilt before God.

In *Counterfeit Gods*, Keller writes, "It is impossible to understand a culture without discerning its idols."[18]   Keller, who is pastor of Redeemer Presbyterian Church in New York City, often speaks about idolatry as the major barrier to the spread of the gospel in a city. He notes that the diversity, restlessness, and tolerance so common in urban areas make them a breeding ground for idols. Indeed, the Bible often identifies a city by its idols, as in the cases of Sodom, Ephesus, and Athens.

Oftentimes, a city's landmarks acknowledge, commemorate, or even celebrate a district's idols and strongholds. Drive through the working class neighborhoods of Belfast, Ireland, and you'll see countless examples. Wall after wall is covered in memorial murals depicting victims of the political and religious conflict the Northern Irish refer to as "The Troubles."

On the surface, painting the side of a building with the likeness of a fallen friend sounds like a noble thing. To be sure, the wounds of The Troubles are fresh and peace is elusive. But the murals serve as constant reminders of wrongs suffered on both sides, and further perpetuate the

---

16 Calvin, *Institutes of the Christian Religion*, 1536.

17 Stetzer, The Upstream Collective Jet Set Vision Trip, Istanbul, Turkey, 2010.

18 Keller, *Counterfeit Gods*, 166.

division, violence, and hate they grieve. Neighbors maintain the murals as ideological shrines, demonstrating their commitment to their side's cause by adorning the sites with photos, flags, curios, and flowers. To an outsider, it would seem that the Northern Irish worship their slain comrades. Maybe the images themselves are not idols, but the bitterness of the grudge certainly may be. In the hearts of Irish people on both sides of the conflict, the stronghold of offense is given the place that rightfully belongs to Jesus.

Cultural exegesis must identify the idols that are worshiped throughout the city. Ephesians 6:12 reminds God's people that their true enemy isn't other people: "For we do not wrestle against flesh and blood, but against the rulers, against the authorities, against the cosmic powers over this present darkness, against the spiritual forces of evil in the heavenly places." A stronghold is any argument or high thing that exalts itself against the knowledge of God (2 Cor. 10:4–5). These may be the lasting memory of wrongdoing, tolerance of sin, the shame of failure, or pride in success.

Potential idols include materialism, sex, power, and wealth. The shrines to these idols are everywhere: shopping malls, billboards, movie theaters, restaurants, and sporting arenas. Observation and personal interactions will reveal these things and help you see how to show their inadequacy to save.

Oftentimes, idols are wrapped up as a culture's values. A people's values can be discovered in many ways, but the least reliable is to ask the people directly. Many people may be unaware of the idols around which they orient their lives. Values are best seen in the behaviors, objects, and systems a culture holds in high regard. These include anything that is important to people. More often than not, values are expressed through how people spend their time, money, and energy.

Jesus challenged the values of the rich young man,[19] saying that not only was his wealth powerless to save him, it was actually the one thing that would prevent him from entering the kingdom. The man willfully chose material riches over eternal salvation and went away sad.

Here, Jesus shows that it isn't enough to simply identify a city's idols, they must be exposed as such. Cultural exegesis provides the information and insight, but the missionary's job is much more than just understanding. In Athens, Paul demonstrated the value of recognizing idolatry (Acts 17) when he confronted the idols worshiped

---

19 Mark 10:17–22.

there. Members of his audience said, "We will hear you again about this" and "some men joined him and believed." In order to make disciples, there must be a call to deliberately leave the service of created things for service to the Most High God.

## Conflict

Another significant cultural element in need of exegesis is conflict. In its most basic sense, conflict involves anyone with whom a people may be at odds. Disagreements, aggression, and war are all examples of conflict, but they are never the extent of conflict. People, since the fall of man, are conflicted internally as well as externally; shame, guilt, offense, fear, and hate are universal human emotions.

In order to find these internal conflicts, we need to build on our observations of a people's values. Conflict arises wherever something challenges the values of a people. A group who worships at the throne of consumerism will take on massive amounts of debt in order to maintain their materialistic lifestyle. People who value their political system above everything else will kill to preserve that system. Threats to family, freedom, religion, and control will almost invariably lead to conflict.

Turkey is a conflicted nation. As a large country that bridges the European and Asian continents, Turkey has a history of war with East and West. Outer conflicts have produced inner conflicts; on the one hand, they are an ancient, Arab-influenced, Muslim nation in the Ottoman tradition. On the other hand, they are a modern, secular democracy with close ties to the West and a strong desire to join the European Union. At every turn, Turks are conflicted for desiring to be the very thing they want to hate.

Defined to a certain extent by these conflicts, the tension can be seen in every area of Turkish life. The call to prayer sounds five times each day, but the cries of the imam are drowned out by hip-hop music in the streets. Modern shopping malls are built around medieval bazaars. Armed aggression against the Kurdish minority rages on in the north. The island of Cyprus is literally split in half between the Greek and Turkish sides. The Turks are a conflicted people.

After the torture and murder of three Christian missionaries to Turkey in 2007,[20] Turkish Christians were emboldened. Tired of being

---

20 Blake, "Turkey Christian missionaries horrifically tortured before killings."

81

bullied, many began to publicly identify themselves as Christ-followers. A young Turkish church planter is on trial for sharing his faith. An older couple has established a beachhead in the form of a coffee shop. A Christian pastor braves ridicule and physical threats every time he walks to his church building. Nevertheless, Turks are coming to faith. It turns out that in the midst of conflict, the gospel of peace with God through Jesus Christ is very good news.

Conflict is universal. When exegeting culture, look for signs of struggle. Extreme poverty, war, oppression, protest, and unrest are clear indications of deep social divides. But there are other, less obvious indications of strife. Often celebrated as positive change, gentrification and explosive growth can be serious flash points for conflict between generations, races, social classes, and ideologies. Where there is conflict, there is hurt, frustration, misunderstanding, and ill-will. Listen for heated rhetoric, outrage, and demonization of one party by another. Of course, it isn't enough for the missionary to observe signs of conflict. In order to live as a preview of the Kingdom, we must interject ourselves as peacemakers. Though it might sound counterintuitive, we do this by finding the weak and oppressed and encouraging them not to seek retribution. Thom Wolf sees a pattern of discipleship throughout the New Testament: the weaker side in any conflict is the one with the power to speak peace into the situation.[21]

Wolf points out that throughout Paul's epistles, he appeals first to the weaker party in the social dynamic and then to the stronger, urging both to respond to one another with grace and forgiveness.[22] Paul addresses five pairs: wives and their husbands, children and their parents, employee and employer, insider and outsider, and Christian and those who are in authority. In each case, Paul's attention to the minority shows that person's ability to control conflict. The cycle of aggression is broken when the victim of oppression responds in forgiveness to his oppressor. Cultural exegesis will reveal the person or group of people who can make peace in the face of violence and unrest.

Cultural exegesis is basic missionary tradecraft. It is a skill learned only through practice, patience, and diligent study. Just as teachers of sound doctrine insist on the thorough study and informed interpretation of Scripture, churches should equip their people to be skilled exegetes of the cultures in which they find themselves.

---

21 Wolf, "Urban Social Change."

22 Wolf, "The Universal Discipleship Pattern."

# EXEGETING CULTURE: HOW-TO

Observe all that you can. Too often, missionaries turn to books or the Internet for research into the customs and cultures of the people to whom they wish to minister. Much can be learned this way, but nothing compares to the field experience you get from examining culture with your own eyes.

**Stories**—Listen to local storytellers, read indigenous literature, watch local television and films. Listen for common themes, popular sentiments, and clues into the culture's perspective on identity in relation to God, creation, and the rest of humanity.

**Space**—Occupy the same space as the people to whom you've been sent. If they gather around campfires, join them. If they hang out in coffee shops, pull up a chair and learn to love coffee. If they live in high-rise apartments, move into the building. To exegete a people's use of space, you must, as far as possible, share that space with them.

**Idols**—Identify whatever it is that people orient their lives around. Discern what people are afraid of. Find what they worship in the place of the Most High God and begin to develop ways to show and tell people that it is better to worship Him.

**Conflict**—Look for sources of tension and unresolved conflict. Usually, people establish rules to deal with conflict.

Ask lots of questions. Rather than assume you know why people do what they do, ask them. This will provide opportunities to build relationships and share the gospel. Learn the story, experience the space, identify the idols, and discover ways to stand for peace in the midst of conflict. Record what you observe, as it may become clear later how these things are bridges or barriers to the gospel.

# BUILDING RELATIONSHIPS

## [chapter 5]

BY RODNEY CALFEE

The gospel is about relationships. The good news is about a King who became like people in order to relate to them, so they might understand who He really is. His desire is for relationship, redeemed and free of encumbrance, and He paid the ultimate price to achieve it.

Jesus talked almost endlessly about relationship—His with His Father,[1] His with His followers,[2] His followers with each other,[3] and His followers with others.[4] The New Testament writers focused on the same emphases, namely God's relationship with His people in and through Christ, their relationships with one another (the Church), and how they related to the world as His ambassadors.

If we are to understand and proclaim the gospel in light of relationship as well, then we must learn all that we can about relationships in general—how to form them, keep them, grow them, and even dissolve them. Particularly, if we are to follow Jesus' instructions to find the person of peace (Luke 10) and leverage his relationships for the spread of the gospel, then relational tools must become a priority.[5]

## Relationship demands a bond

Bonds connect people in relationship, whether good, bad, or indifferent. Blood relation, friendship, life stages, hobbies, affinity, dislikes—all of these are connectors. They are the seeds of relationship. Every relationship has at least one connector, and the deeper a relationship goes, the more connectors exist.

For instance, two guys who are lifelong friends have likely thousands of connectors in the form of shared memories and experiences that trace back to the first time they played t-ball together at age four. Co-workers are connected around common business goals and a shared office space. Surfers are connected around their passion for the sport and the pursuit of the perfect wave. Green Bay Packers fans

---

1 John 5:19–23, 36–37; 6:57; 8:16, 19, 28; 10:15, 25–30; 13:31; 14:11–14; 15:1, 9–10, 23; 16:3, 28; 17:1–5, 10, 21–26, et al.

2 John 1:43; 3:18; 4:13; 6:25–29, 35–37; 6:67–70; 7:37–38; 8:12, 36; 9:39; 10.9–16, 27–28; 12:44–48; 14:1–3, 6, 23; 15:9–11; 16:16–24; 17:7–9, 20–24, et al.

3 Matthew 5:21–26; 18:15–20; 20:26–28; John 13:14–15, 33–34; 17:21, et al.

4 Matthew 5:11, 16, 21–48; 6:1–5; 7:1–5, 12; 10:5–24, 40–42; 18:1–6, 15–35; 20:26–28; 22:39; 28:18–20, et al.

5 More on this idea in chapters, "Identifying Persons of Peace" and "Engaging Tribes."

are connected around cheese-shaped head coverings and giant green and yellow foam fingers.

Even enemies have a relational connector. They have experienced something in their history over which they have disagreed so vehemently that it has caused them to be tied in a hate-filled relationship. It is around that experience that their relationship exists and by which they are inextricably tied.

## God is relational

When we read God's story, we quickly learn that Jesus is good at relationship. He looks for points of connection and takes advantage of them. He pays attention to who people are and develops relationships based on what He knows of them.[6] His followers should do the same. We should work hard to develop relational skills, because the gospel is built on relationship. It is through relationships that it will continue to spread.

We are called to relationship with God the Father through Christ. God has always existed in community, and we reflect the same communal character[7]. Theologian, author, and professor Millard Erickson wrote about the effect on the church of understanding God as communal (triune) in his book on Trinitarian theology. He wrote, "It would seem that a first implication would be . . . that true personhood involves social interaction, social relationships. To the extent that the individual reflects the image of the Triune God, that individual would

---

6 The story of the woman at the well in John 4 is a perfect example of this. Jesus used what He knew of the woman to gain her trust and build relationship with her. He understood her and was therefore able to give her the good news of living water that applied directly to her situation.

7 The doctrine of the Trinity teaches that God exists eternally as three persons who are each fully God, and there is one God. The word Trinity does not appear in Scripture, but we see the Trinity revealed throughout Scripture—Genesis 1:2, 26; John 1:1–3—the Trinity in creation; Matthew 3:16–17—at Jesus' baptism; Matthew 28:19–20—sending the Church; 1 Corinthians 12: 4–6—empowering the Church; Jude 20–21—as the foundation of our faith; et al. Trinitarian ideas of community gleaned from the oneness of God also inform the manner in which the church builds relationships. The lessons learned from God-in-community are commonly and appropriately applied to marriage, family, and the church, mainly built around the central idea of many being unified as one, not in uniformity, but as multiple distinct persons operating in unique roles with unique gifts moving with one purpose toward the same end—Ephesians 4:1–16; 5:22–6:9; 1 Corinthians 12:4–31.

not be solitary or independent, but would be related to other persons . . . in a particular way."[8] Since we are made in the image of God, we, too, are communal.

The Scriptures describe the myriad appropriate ways in which we relate to God and He relates to us. He is creator, and we revere Him as such. He is our healer, and we come to Him in brokenness. He is redeemer, so we come to Him to be made new. He is provider, lover, defender, forgiver, shepherd, and judge, and we relate to Him in a manner befitting His character.

For instance, God is holy, so we cannot approach Him in our sin. Instead, He has pursued us and made a way for payment of our debt through Christ's life, death, and resurrection. We are cleansed of sin and are given Christ's righteousness in order to reconcile our sinfulness to God's holiness (Rom. 3:21–26; 2 Cor. 5:21). We relate to God, then, by way of understanding as best we can who He is and approaching Him according to what we know of Him.

No one approaches a king with a list of demands; instead, in humility and meekness, when beckoned by the king, one approaches and begs for mercy. In the same way, we relate to God, whom we also know is infinitely merciful toward those He has called. We relate to Him through His incarnate Son, Emmanuel—God with us. But we can do so only because Jesus came to us, walked in relationship with us, and experienced every temptation we do. He related to us, so that we can relate to Him. All of it was for relationship, God drawing man unto Himself as a part of his great redemptive plan.

Consider the great stories of Scripture—Abraham's call out of Ur, Moses' call to rescue God's people from Pharaoh in Egypt, Joshua's call to take them into the Promised Land, the prophets who spoke for God, Peter's brave obedience in taking the gospel to Cornelius' house, and Paul's defiant demeanor when he determined that he would serve the Lord even in chains. Each of these stories is for the redemptive purpose of relationship – that people would know "the only true God, and Jesus Christ whom [He has] sent."[9] Their purpose is for us to have a redeemed relationship with God.

---

8 Erickson, *God in Three Persons*, 332–333.

9 John 17:3.

## The church is relational

Believers also relate to one another in a familial manner[10]. The New Testament authors continually and purposefully referred to the believers as brothers and God as Father,[11] spoke of our reconciliation to God that made us a part of His household[12] through adoption,[13] and taught that we should love each other like a family.[14]

Paul taught that in God's family the distinctions and divisions have fallen away. There is no male, no female, no slave, no free, no Jew nor Greek.[15] We are one, related through the blood of Christ. Our relationship is defined. We relate via the body and blood of Christ. Our differences melt away in light of the cross.

The gospel is the unifying principle for those in the church to relate to one another. We unite as sinners who have experienced the forgiveness of Christ and been cleansed by His blood. We are part of one body, so we should relate to one another as such.[16] We certainly still have much work to do in actually relating to one another in the prescribed manner, but at least our unifying principle of relation is understood.

Less clear to many within the church, however, is how we are to be in relationship with people who are not believers, people who do not understand or have rejected the basic relational principle upon which our relationships within the body are built. There are diverging approaches on the matter, ranging from isolationism to syncretistic inclusion and everything between. The extremes are obvious theological error, but there is much space between them in which most believers find themselves, and these are often waters not easily navigated.

The largest barrier in building relationships with people who are not part of God's family is they do not operate according to His standards. The common unifying factor in Christian relationships doesn't unite us with unbelievers because they don't believe or act "like us." But, why would they? We must remember that we did not believe

---

10 Mark 3:33–35.

11 Colossians 1:2.

12 Galatians 4:28,31; Ephesians 2:19.

13 Galatians 4:4–7.

14 Romans 12:10; 1 Timothy 5:1–2; 1 John 2:9–11; 5:2.

15 Romans 10:12; 1 Corinthians 12:13; Galatians 3:28; Colossians 3:11.

16 1 Corinthians 12; Ephesians 4–6.

or act "like us" before God saved us, either. In many cases, it is as though the Church has forgotten that we were once unable to relate to God. We were His enemies, and Christ had to come to us in order to reconcile us to God (Rom. 5:10).

God prescribed a way that we should interact with each other within His body, and it should inform the manner in which we relate to outsiders, as well. The overarching characteristic was and now remains love. In Deuteronomy 4, Moses began restating and expounding upon the Law that God had given His people as a directive on how to live together among the nations. Their obedience to the Law was to be a beacon of righteousness that would cause the surrounding peoples to see the greatness of God (Deut. 4:5–8). The greatest command in the Law was love (Deut. 6:5).

Jesus echoed the same sentiment, teaching that the greatest commandment was to love God, and the second was to love others (Mark 12:28–34). He also told the disciples love would be the characteristic mark of His disciples (John 13:33–34). The way they loved one another would show the world that they were His. For their infectious love to be noticed by the world, they must be near the world in relationship, hence Jesus' prayer to the Father was that He not take them out of the world, but guard them from the evil one (John 17:14–18).

Unfortunately, too often the church's approach is to demand that outsiders live according to a moral code by which they gain relationship to us and, by proxy, to God (i.e., abstain from sex, drugs, and hard rock ,and we can be friends). Instead of building meaningful relationships with outsiders through which they may see God's character reflected in and through us (imperfect as it may be), we demand a holiness from the world that no one can employ apart from the grace of God.

Few of us would ever say that out loud; we just act that way by befriending people who are "less immoral" than others and condemning the "more immoral" for not living up to a code of ethics to which they do not even ascribe. This is a steep divergence from the Jesus we follow who was called a friend of sinners by the "righteous" (Luke 7:34).

The truth is this: The people of God are not related solely on affinity but on the common experience of the gospel. We have been forgiven (Col. 1:14), cleansed (2 Pet. 1:9), adopted (Gal. 4:4–7), given new names—a common name (Eph. 3:15), and sent to represent the One whose name we now bear (2 Cor 5.18-20). The Scriptures never demand that we relate to one another (unify) based on the fact that we really like to hang out. We unify around a common Savior and a common mission, neither of which is shared in common with people outside of God's family. So we must be good relationship-builders based on other external factors.

# MAKING FRIENDS IS GOOD: HOW-TO

Being able to make friends is an important tool for people on mission. Though it sounds simplistic, it is important to note that building relationships is of highest importance and it does not come naturally to a number of people. The awkward nature of developing friendships causes many people, Christians included, to avoid it. That is not helpful.

I am an introvert. I enjoy crowds, as long as I know most of the people in them or I am in front of them. (I must admit that I like being on stage—a confession of sorts.) However, when it comes to new people, I don't naturally relate. I have to work hard to find some commonality on which to focus. I don't do small talk very well, so if I don't zero in on something common I will crash and burn quickly. Therefore, it is good for me to have a few tools at my disposal for relationship building.

I am not alone in my social ineptitude. So the following are several tools to use in relationship building. It is by no means an exhaustive list, but one that may be a helpful start:

## 1. People are not targets; they are God's image-bearers

People are not targets for our efforts or the object of our tasks. Each is made in God's image and therefore worthy of and made for relationship, just as we are. We must be careful to treat them as such.

People need and desire relationships, even introverts like me, and relationship-building is a part of who we are as ambassadors (2 Corinthians 5.11–21). Reconciliation requires it. As we build relationships, we need to take care with our language. How we describe people and how we talk about them will shape how we treat them.

Think about a close friend. Consider how you think, feel, talk about, and treat him. Now contrast him with how you treat someone you don't really know, like the teller at the bank or the guy who always bags your groceries or the woman from whom you buy your coffee every day. The way you label people often determines the way you treat them. Consider a commonly practiced version of evangelism. First, people are the "lost." They hear and believe the gospel and they are labeled "new Christians." They begin to grow and become "people you are discipling."

In both local and global mission, it is easy for terms like "souls saved" to portray people in terms of numbers on a ledger sheet. But when do they simply become your friends? When does he move from "some lost guy" to "my friend, Roger"? Jesus certainly thought such a distinction was important. In John 15:15, Jesus said, "No longer do I call you servants, for the servant does not know what his master is doing; but I have called you friends, for all that I have heard from my Father I have made known to you."

His disciples were His friends because He had shared with them the truth. Similarly, our role as ambassadors is to share the truth about God in Christ—to bear witness to the light (John 1:7–8). According to Jesus' words, we do that with our friends, people we love. This is not just semantics. Words are important. Words define things. By our words, we define people. We can either treat them as others worthy of relationship or sentence them to life as a project to be completed.

If we choose the latter, our expectation should be that people would respond accordingly. I am not advocating for an all-out ousting of all descriptive terminology; I am simply suggesting we must be careful that our labels do not cause us to treat people in a way not conducive to building honest relationships with them. As much as we can do so, we need to avoid labels and categorizations altogether. As soon as we assume that we have someone figured out, we stop learning about him and the relationship is hindered.

## 2. The gospel should be shared in context of relationship

Relationships garner trust, which is a necessity for an appropriate transmission of the gospel. In fact, there are a couple of common colloquialisms that speak to that fact generally, and evangelism specifically:

"You must earn the right to be heard."

"Before you share, I need to know you care."

These statements though a bit trite point to a valid truth. Since we are relational creatures in the image of God, the proper context for gospel cultivation is relationship. Often, however, believers ask for this kind of trust from the world without first proving that we really do care —without getting to know them, their hurts, passions, and needs.

In such cases, people aren't necessarily rejecting the gospel so much as they are rejecting the way we are presenting it. If we know nothing about those to whom we are sent, we cannot know how the gospel is good news to them. The gospel is always good news, but how it is good to a particular individual depends on who he is. To assume can be dangerous and may even end in an ignorant rejection of truth based on a misunderstanding of what it actually is.

The good news to the Samaritan woman at the well was very different than the good news to the official whose son Jesus healed a few days later (John 4). Each instance was couched in Jesus' understanding of those He was sent to, what their needs were, and what the good news was to them. The result in each instance was that not only the individual to whom Jesus went, but also his household believed in Him as the Messiah.

We must take the time to know the ones to whom we are sent, so that the gospel is shared in the context of relationship. Consider the difference in your initial reaction when a trusted friend asks you for $10 versus your reaction when a beggar on the street does the same. The determining factor for your response is relationship. The same principle applies when we share the gospel. The proper context for gospel cultivation is relationship.

### 3. Don't assume you already know. Ask questions

"For by the grace given to me I say to everyone among you not to think of himself more highly than he ought to think, but to think with sober judgment, each according to the measure of faith that God has assigned," said Paul in Romans 12:3. Having been a Pharisee, Paul knew what it was to have all the answers and to have "confidence in the flesh" (Phil. 3:4–7). He was a teacher of the law and from the evidence in the gospels, the Pharisees' only questions were meant either to prove that they knew more than others or to somehow lay a trap for Jesus and His followers (Mark 12:13–14; Luke 5:21). So Paul admonished the Roman believers to watch out for their pride.

His admonition is well received among believers today, assuming we are able to personally determine exactly how highly we ought to think of ourselves. We tend toward pride, like the Pharisees, and most of us really like to have the answers. Usually, the one with the answers is the one who ends up in charge.

Jesus obviously knew the answers and regularly taught prescriptively by asking a lot of questions. He did not always offer the answers freely but routinely invited others into the conversation. In doing so, He recognized and affirmed their value as image-bearers whose response was worth hearing. He lovingly corrected answers not in line with the truth and led many to follow Him in that truth.

On the other hand, the church's primary approach is often toward apologetics, trying to defend truth through reason rather than offering Christ's love through relationship. A thorough defense of the faith is often needed; but when it occurs in Scripture, it is in opposition to false teaching within the church,[17] not outside.

Our posture toward those outside the church should be one of love, not of antagonism, a position we can quickly assume when we determine that we must prove them wrong in order to win them over. People do not need a defense of God; they need to experience His character through His representatives. We must be careful not to assume an adversarial position and portray God as adversarial in the process.

One way we can help to ensure the proper posture is by asking questions and listening well to the answers. By doing so, we are able to learn who people are and what the good news is to them. We cannot learn about them by prescribing what they need to know. We learn whom people are by asking them to tell us. Then, we listen. They will tell us how we should share the gospel in a manner that is relevant and powerful in their lives.[18]

I remember the first time I met her. Ms. Debbie, or so we'll call her, was the community "grandmother." Everyone knew her and she knew everyone. She knew everyone's business, too. She had lived in the same government housing community for more than 50 years. She was a sweet woman, and opened her home to me after only a couple of conversations.

I had been trying to do ministry within the community, which was just a few blocks from my local church's building for about a year when

---

17 Jude 3–4; Acts 15; Gal 5.1–12.

18 I am not discounting the power of the Spirit to give us insight into the lives and needs of others; we should certainly pray and ask for wisdom. However, since we are relational creatures, intended to move in relationship, we need to learn to take advantage of the natural ways God created us to connect with others.

I met her. Just like many of the others I had met, I assumed a lot about Ms. Debbie. The main assumption I made was about what she needed. She needed to move out of that development. To move out, she needed a good job, which would require an alternative high school diploma and a good connection with someone important. I thought I would proclaim good news to her by helping her accomplish those things.

She and I talked a lot, and we spent a lot of time together talking about her community and the people in it. Nevertheless, years later I realized my prescribed good news wasn't good news to Ms. Debbie at all. She had heard it all before from other church people who came in promising to help her do the same things I was promising.

If I had been paying closer attention, asking questions, and listening more to her instead of telling her what she and her community needed, I would have realized that the good news to her was much simpler. Although she knew everyone, she lacked real friendship. She was lonely. She didn't want to get out of the community; it was the only home she could remember and all of the people she cared the most about were there.

Perhaps if I had only listened more and talked less, prescribed less, and assumed less I might have been able to be a good friend. My children might have been able to play in her living room as my wife and I listened to the myriad stories of her life that she wanted so badly to share with someone who wanted to hear them. Instead, my assumptions impeded my ability to really bring the good news of Jesus to a woman desperately in need of Him. A few good questions and a listening ear would have enabled me to be a good friend to her, giving the good news traction in our relationship.

We must remember that relationships are a long-term investment. They require care and effort to grow. They are two-way, and we cannot force them. Relationships only develop as quickly as both people want to move. No matter how charming, culturally sensitive, and funny we are; no matter how well we listen; no matter how much other people like us, if they don't want relationship, we won't have it. We can only develop our side of the relationship. We must give it time.

Any relationship you might have is a gift from God. He has brought to you the people in your life. Be thankful for those relationships and be a good steward of those gifts. Spend time praying over them. Think about them and brainstorm creative ways that you might be able to spend more time with them. Learn about the things they like, and take full advantage of the gift of friends (Matt. 25.13–30).

## 4. Avoid the bait-and-switch

Don't be a friend to anyone just so he will become a believer. If people are worth the relationship because they are created in God's image, then they are worth it whether they ever follow Jesus or not. We should treat others the way we would wish to be treated, and there is nothing in any of us that wants to endure a relationship with an underlying, unknown, or hidden motive.

I heard about a missionary who was on the mission field in a certain area for several years. There he built a friendship with a man based on affinity. They had common interests and became very close because of them. Several years into their friendship, the missionary's time in the area was coming to a close. Before he left, he took his friend to coffee and shared the most urgent and powerful presentation of the gospel he could muster. He told his friend this news was so important he couldn't possibly leave without sharing it.

The friend listened patiently and intently as the missionary shared the story of Jesus. As he finished the story and the time came to leave, the missionary's friend had but one question for him. The missionary hoped his friend would ask how to follow Jesus and what he must do to be saved and leaned in ready to respond. To the missionary's dismay, instead of the question he so desperately wanted to hear, his friend simply asked why, if it was so important, had the missionary waited until then to share this story with him. The timing of this dialogue caused the missionary's friend to question whether or not the friendship had been valid for all of those years.

Bait-and-switch is dangerous. It builds friendship on false pretense and leaves no room for conversations about really important things without the awkward out-of-nowhere spiritual "attack." As well, it calls into question the validity of the prior relationship, as we have just seen. Instead of building relationships on false pretenses, we should be honest about who we are. That does not mean wearing a WWJD T-shirt or giving out "Testamints" all the time. It means living out the character of Christ as prescribed in Scripture, that men may see our good works and glorify our father in heaven (Matt. 5:13–16).

We do not need to be afraid to fully engage in honest relationship with people—relationship that affords us the opportunity to give an account for the hope we have in Christ (1 Peter 3:15). We must be careful, though, not to develop friendships simply as a means to preach, but instead to share "not only the gospel of God, but also our own selves."[19] The people to whom we are sent are worth pouring our lives into, the result of which will be more opportunity for them to see Christ in us and hear the grace-filled words of the gospel proclaimed in our interactions.

## 5. Be a blessing

Maybe being a blessing is a given, but I'll go ahead and mention it nonetheless. The result of the original covenant with Abraham was that the world would be blessed through him and his lineage.[20] The fact that we are ambassadors and therefore represent Christ in the world means we are messengers of good news. Good news is in its very nature good for those who receive it. Ambassadors of good news should then bless the people around them. Surprisingly, people who are blessed tend to be open to deeper relationship with the one who blessed them.

## 6. Be an interesting person

Being interesting draws the attention of other people. They are intrigued and drawn in. No one ever looks for the most boring person in the room and runs over to spend time with him. People like to be with others who tell good stories, enjoy life, and are passionate about something. Christians should be the best at all of those things. We have the best story to tell. Because of that story, we should enjoy our lives immensely. In fact, Jeff Vanderstelt, founding pastor of the Soma Communities says that Christians should throw the best parties, because we have something real to celebrate.[21] Because of these things, our passion for Christ and His kingdom should be evident to those around us. Christians should be creative, fun, passionate, enjoyable, and interesting people. Be one.

Here are a few keys to helping you be interesting along the way:

**Be a witness.** You don't have a witness so much as you are a witness to the most amazing story in history. You are a witness to the light that

---

19 1 Thessalonians 2:8.

20 Genesis 12:3.

21 Vanderstelt, "Why Throwing Parties is Missional."

shines in the darkness and overcomes it (John 1:7–8). You are a witness of what Jesus has done, and more specifically, how He has redeemed you. When people speak of having a witness, often they are concerned with morality, which is not a bad thing in and of itself. Christians are certainly to be moral people, but that does not equate to being a witness. A witness is one who has particular knowledge of something or someone of interest; it is one who has experienced someone or something of importance. Hence, John said he was a witness of the true Light and he spoke about Him. In word and deed, we are to be witnesses of the Light. People will not see Jesus in us because of our morality. There are plenty of moral people who don't have a clue who Jesus is. We are not to be known by what we don't do, we are to be known by our love, a love we learned from Jesus (John 13.34).

**Remember people's names.** Write them down. Put them in your phone. Carry a little notebook and make notes when you can. Be crafty —snap a picture with your phone while they're not looking and enter them as a contact in your address book. Do what it takes to remember. Also, as you make note of people's names, pay close attention to the pronunciation, especially in a foreign culture. In doing so, you may avoid a little embarrassment and gain yourself a little credibility as an acceptable outsider next time you meet. I confess I am horrible at remembering names, so I have to be intentional if I am going to remember them. But what an incredible moment when I can surprise someone who does not expect me to remember his name (or doesn't remember yours) by simply remembering who he is, shaking his hand, and speaking his name. This gesture shows I value him enough to make sure I remember who he is and helps me gain credibility as I begin to build a new relationship.

**Remember the conversations you have had.** As important as remembering people's names is remembering who they are, what they do, and anything else they have offered in conversation. If they have trusted you with some information about themselves, don't lightly discard it. Relationship is costly, and most people do not give away information for free. If they see that you've mishandled information they have told you already, they will be far less likely to offer anything new.

Recalling a former conversation and asking for updates is one of the easiest ways to make conversation with a new friend, particularly in the awkward beginnings of a relationship. So remember! If necessary, keep a log of your new friends. Record their name, personal information, and any pertinent information regarding what was going on in their life the last time you spoke with them. If you do so, you can ask about it later and show that it mattered to you.

**Pay attention to how you look.** If you dress like a foreigner, it only stresses the differences between you and those around you. Don't imagine that this difference will only be noticed in another country, either. You are a foreigner in any culture other than your own, not just one across an ocean. Certainly, there are differences in dress between a Southern American man and a Sudanese man in their respective cultures; but there are also differences between a Southern American lawyer and a Southern American biker. (I'm drawing on stereotypes here, of course. I know some lawyers who ride motorcycles).

Even apart from the extremes, tribes tend to have a common style of dress, and in some tribes, the style of dress is important enough to exclude others on its merits. Some differences you may not even notice if you aren't paying close attention can even cause the ones to whom you are sent to be embarrassed to be seen with you. That tends to be a major hindrance to building a relationship. So do your best to minimize your physical differences and maximize your spiritual ones.

You want tribe members to see the difference in the attitudes and character of a believer, not the differences in appearance between your tribe and theirs. God's call to a new culture might include wearing jeans that don't fit the way you'd like or having to wear your favorite baggy sweatshirt only in the house. Be yourself, but be a version of yourself that embraces the cultural nuance around you.

Being countercultural as a believer does not mean being anti-local fashion. It means garnering the character of a believer among people who do not believe. Moses taught the Israelites that developing godly character according to the Law had deep missiological implications. The character of God's people would cause the nations to stand in awe of God's nearness to them and to ask, ". . . what great nation is there, that has statutes and rules so righteous as all of this law?"[22] Paul taught the same ideas to the church. He said that external cultural things like circumcision or food sacrificed to idols did not determine who they were and could therefore be forsaken or upheld for the sake of mission.[23] What made them countercultural in his estimation was their

---

22 Deuteronomy 8:5–8.

23 Galatians 5:2–6; Acts 16:3; 1 Corinthians 8.

character, which exposed the state of their hearts.[24] Therefore, we need to be culturally aware enough to dress the part in order to avoid potential roadblocks on mission.[25]

**Live among the people; live like the people**. Jesus came to us, as one of us, in order to relate to us (Phil. 2; Heb. 4:15). He then sent us out in the same way He had been sent (John 20:21). Therefore, we enter the culture of the people we are sent to. We become like them and live among them. Like Jesus, though, who became like us and lived among us yet was without sin, we also do not take part in sin. We take up the pieces and parts of our surrounding culture that are not inherently sinful, such as language, dress, diet, and schedule. An important part of removing barriers to new friendships and doing things like the people around you exposes common interests and makes you more interesting to them.

## Conversational Tools

Conversation is a key tool for building relationships. It is important to be able to communicate well who you are, as well as to understand who your new friends are. Countless books on building relationships are available. This is not an attempt at writing one of our own. However, there are a few things to remember when engaging someone, particularly someone new, in conversation.

## 1. Listen

Listen to the other person instead of just waiting for your turn to talk. One of the most damaging and annoying practices of conversation is when one of the participants is obviously not paying attention, because he is too distracted thinking about what he will say next. Stop it. Listen. Engage. Even if you don't get to say anything, be sure to really care about what your new friend is saying. If you don't pay attention now, you will never remember what he has said to you so that you can further a conversation later.

---

24 Galatians 5:16–26; Colossians 3:5–17.

25 More on this in the chapter, "Contextualization."

## 2. Pay attention

Remember that your posture and responses show whether or not you're paying attention. Looking beyond your friend at the television in the corner, losing yourself in the traffic going by, or allowing yourself to be distracted by something on your cell phone are dead giveaways that you are not engaged. Adopt the culturally-appropriate posture that communicates that you are listening. The goal is to demonstrate that you care by showing that you are paying close attention.

## 3. Read the person you are talking to

If he isn't listening or paying attention to you, stop talking. Notice his body language and don't force anyone to listen to you. You probably know what it is to have someone continue talking when you've lost interest. Pay close attention so you do not do the same thing to him.

## 4. Don't just talk about religion

Not every conversation has to be about Jesus. All of your conversations with your other friends aren't, so they don't need to be with your new friends either. Find conversation stimulants about life, common interests, and pop culture. Watch television and movies. Listen to music and read books. Look for truth amidst regular conversation. It's also okay to disagree, so you don't necessarily have to avoid touchy or sensitive subjects. Your opinions, thoughts, and actions will all be deeply affected by Christ, so it is okay to talk about them. This does not mean you are not having Christ-centered conversations. Your conversations about family, friendship, work, and social endeavors will all expose the Lordship of Jesus in your life and become natural bridges to deeper spiritual conversations.

## 5. Be real

Being real is a difficult concept for people who don't already know how. Be honest. Share your thoughts, struggles, concerns, passions, doubts, wins, and losses. People identified with the humanity of Jesus, so we should show ours as well. Don't lie and say everything is all right if it isn't. At the same time don't unload all your troubles on some unsuspecting person. You are supposed to be ministering to them. Your support is found in Christ and His church.

## On Purpose

Living on mission doesn't happen accidentally. It requires intentionality, planning, and even practice. Everything you do should leave the mark of Jesus. Make good choices and operate according to the leadership of the Spirit. "Let your light shine, so they may see your good works and give glory to Your Father in Heaven" (Matt. 5:16). Interestingly, what it does not say is, "Make sure you tell them what's good, point out that you're doing it, and make sure to tell them why."

Show others Jesus' character in your actions. Live with them and let them in on your life. They need to see, hear, feel, and experience you as you live as a light among them. They need to see you growing in your faith, as they grow in theirs. You are a fellow traveler along the road to spiritual maturity. Be creative and build relationships that will lead to other relationships along the way.

Finally, begin with the end in mind. This old adage can be used of many endeavors in our lives, including building relationships. Sometimes it is necessary for relationships to change. If we have friends who have come to follow Jesus and are working among their friends and within their own culture, there may come a time when we need to step away from them and what they are doing to preserve indigeneity within their local expression of the church. This is actually a good thing, because it means the gospel is spreading and the church is growing. There may also come a time when relationships are not healthy or even become adversarial, and we must make the difficult choice to walk away (Luke 10:10–16). Although such action is not what we prefer, it is sometimes necessary. Therefore, prepare yourself in advance for changing relationships and pray for wisdom as to how you will graciously walk through such change.

The ability to build relationships, to be a good ambassador and friend is a necessary part of missionary tradecraft. Some people are gifted with an innate ability to relate to people. Others of us must develop the skill. Either way, this is a skill that cannot be overlooked as we engage our neighbors and the nations on mission.

# IDENTIFYING PERSONS OF PEACE

## [chapter 6]

BY RODNEY CALFEE

Let's say you need a job and you just heard of one that has come open. Your resume is polished, and you are more than qualified for the position. At the outset, it appears you are golden—nothing is lacking. You ready yourself to hit "submit" on the Web page to send your resume into cyberspace when you remember that your first cousin's best friend is a low-level manager in the company to which you are applying. She is well-respected and climbing the ladder within the company, so a recommendation from her would give you an extra boost. It would be far more impressive if she hand-delivered your resume to the decision makers as a personal referral. You quickly back the cursor away in favor of adding the one thing a perfect resume can never accomplish—the power of relationship.

### Enchufe

In Spanish, the word used for this type of relationship is *enchufe*. The literal translation of the word is "plug," but it is used metaphorically to describe a connection or inroad. It implies that one person is "pulling strings" for another and assisting him in achieving the desired outcome. An *enchufe* is a good thing. Jobs, relationships, and various opportunities become reality through the help of a relational connector.

The *enchufe* is common among other cultures, as well. American culture certainly understands the importance of a relational mediator. The reason this concept is a familiar one is simple—relationships define us. We were made for community. "Let us make man in our image," said the One who created all things (Gen.1:26). As God has eternally existed in relationship, we were made to enjoy and exist in relationship (Mark 12:30–31; John 17:21–23). Jesus even talked about the power of our relationships in revealing the truth of the gospel to the world (13:34–35; John 17:21–23).

The simple reality is that people want to be in relationship with other people, and existing relationships are powerful tools for creating new relationships. They are often leveraged[1] for creating opportunities that otherwise would not have existed. As the old adage goes, "It's not what you know, but who you know that matters."

People research and learn through relationship, taking on a bit of a guinea pig-like quality. Here are a few examples you might hear or ask:

- One friend asks another, "How is the food at (insert restaurant here)? I was thinking about trying it out . . ."
- At the playground, one mother comments to another, "We need a new pediatrician. How do you like yours?"
- Facebook status update: Who knows a good mechanic? Major car troubles over here . . .
- When discussing an upcoming backpacking trip, one hiker asks another, "What kind of hiking shoes do you use?"
- As the numbers on the gas pump race higher and higher, a young father asks the person at the next pump, "Do you like your car? How's the gas mileage?"
- After a show, a young concert attendee asks the headlining guitarist, "What type of effects pedals do you use?"
- Tweet: Which Twitter app do you use for the iPhone? I don't like the one I have. Looking for a new one.

Technically, all of the information we need can usually be found online, in phone books, magazines, and product reviews, but we would rather hear the thoughts of someone to whom we already relate, someone we know and trust. For instance, I was in the market for new hiking boots several years ago and began to read reviews about several different kinds. Not knowing the people writing them, I didn't really know whether or not to trust their opinions. Their reviews in mind, I went boot shopping with a friend who is an experienced hiker and knows the trouble I have had with boots in the past. I tried on several

---

1 "Leverage" is a terrible word to use when speaking of relationship. However, it is the right word to use in this case, as long as we stray from a distinctly utilitarian understanding of the term. In its simplest form, it means "to use for gain." People often meet other people through existing relationships. Understanding that to be so, we can take advantage of the process — not the people — and intentionally use existing relationships to build other relationships. I am not advocating we use people simply to find an avenue to other friends. I am instead suggesting that we understand how relationships breed other relationships, and allow this natural avenue to develop fertile soil for the gospel. That is not utility; it is friendship and stewardship.

different styles and ended up buying a pair that received less than stellar reviews in an outdoor magazine simply because my friend suggested that I try them on. They were precisely what I needed.

As this story illustrates, people often depend on relationship over and above conventional wisdom. Based on the recommendation of others, we will be open to something or someone we otherwise would not have considered. Advertisers know this to be true, hence all the recognizable faces and stories in ads and commercials. They want the audience to relate, to connect with people and their stories, and as a result, to the product they are selling. To do this, they invoke the power of relationship and referral.

Think about things you've bought, watched, read, or listened to, places you've visited, or would like to. How many of those are because of the testimony of someone you relate to — not only someone you know, but also someone you feel like you know — a celebrity or a storyteller in a commercial? For many of us, the percentage is likely pretty high. We were made for relationship, and it shows.

Referral is important to us; even businesses know it. Think of all of the referral programs offered by banks, credit card companies, and cell phone services. These programs make our friends spokespeople for their products and services. They work because we are made for relationship, and our relationships deeply influence the decisions we make.

The same is true for things much more important than consumeristic pursuits, such as the type of shoes you wear or the car you drive. Relationship determines what and whom you believe, as well. You trust the local mechanic because your brother-in-law, who you trust already, told you he was trustworthy. Your neighbor's wonderful recommendation of her dermatologist has you filling out crossword puzzles in his waiting room. You even allow your best friend's high school buddy who is now a missionary in Bangladesh to share with your family about what it means to follow Jesus, trusting all the while that your friend was right about him. You make all of these decisions based primarily on the reputation and referral of your friends and family, and you are not alone in this practice.

## Person of Peace

Relationship is currency, and there is always a broker.[2] There is always someone who oversees the transaction and on whose word and reputation the exchange hangs. In Luke 10, we read the story of Jesus sending out the 70 (or 72, depending on the translation). Verses 5–9 are as follows:

> 5 Whatever house you enter, first say, 'Peace be to this house!' 6 And if a son of peace is there, your peace will rest upon him. But if not, it will return to you. 7 And remain in the same house, eating and drinking what they provide, for the laborer deserves his wages. Do not go from house to house. 8 Whenever you enter a town and they receive you, eat what is set before you. 9 Heal the sick in it and say to them, 'The kingdom of God has come near to you.'

From this passage, we understand the powerful concept of a person of peace in missional advancement. Jesus prescribed a particular manner in which His followers should approach unfamiliar communities and local cultures. His plan was for His people to go to a given town and "speak peace" to the people there, wait for a response, and act accordingly. If a positive response were given, the follower of Jesus would set up camp in the house of the respondent and work among the community from its vantage point. A negative response required a pronouncement that God's Kingdom had indeed been near, and a warning that refusal to acknowledge that truth and receive the kingdom had dire consequences.[3]

At first, this seems like a strange and overly simplistic directive. Go into a town full of people you don't know and proclaim the same message the angels proclaimed at Christ's birth—the gospel—the good news of the advent of the Kingdom of peace. Wait for a response, and if

---

2 Here again is a strange term for this conversation. "Currency" most commonly has an ascribed utilitarian/financial meaning. It is defined as "a medium of exchange," which can have a plethora of meanings. As with my use of "leverage," we do not promote using people. We do not form a relationship with person A in order to access person B. However, being in relationship with person A may yield the fruit of connection with person B.

3 This particular instruction from Jesus for the disciples He was sending out can also be found in Matthew 10:11–14 and Mark 6:10–11.

a son of peace is found, stay with him.[4] Eat and drink what is set before you. Don't bounce around from place to place. Dwell there, and represent God's Kingdom well within that home. It will be from that home that your ministry within the town will be done.

Certainly, Jesus knew that people were made for relationship. It was, after all, Jesus who made them that way. So, His admonition was to leverage relationship for the sake of the mission through the person of peace. Since this person was of great importance to Christ, we need to endeavor to understand what exactly a person of peace is and why he or she was so important.

Thomas Wolf, defines the person of peace: "'Person of peace' is a Hebraism meaning 'one inclined to peace' (Plummer 1909:273). A person of peace is someone or some group sovereignly prepared by God to receive the gospel."[5]

The person of peace is one already primed, by grace, through the work of the Spirit to receive the good news of Jesus. The presence of such a person speaks to God's sovereignty, having prepared beforehand those who would be saved and softening an otherwise hard heart to the

---

4 We have chosen to use the ESV version of the Bible for quotations within this book. The ESV translates the Greek word υιος as "son," which is a perfectly acceptable translation of the word (though other translations use "person of peace," "peaceful person," or "person who promotes peace"). There are, however, many uses of the word in the New Testament, some representing familial connection, some connoting maleness, some speaking of friends, some speaking broadly about people who act a certain way. It is not a term that necessarily means a male offspring (there are several other Greek words that mean direct relation). υιος is a term that stresses the character of the relationship. It seems in Luke 10 that Jesus means to express the nature of the relationship. The "son of peace" is one who would relate to the sent one as a family member would; they would be accepted, cared for, and taken in as if they belonged to the family of the person of peace. Looking at the examples throughout the New Testament of people who seem to fall into this category, we do not find it helpful to designate the particularly male term "son" for the role. Since it is not used only to delineate maleness in Scripture, we find the use of the term "person of peace" to be appropriate. For more information on this please refer to: W.E. Vines, *An Expository Dictionary of New Testament Words*. Old Tappan: Fleming H. Revell, 1966, Vol 1, 187, Vol 4, 47.

5 As you will note throughout this chapter, much is made here of Wolf's writing. That is, in part, because there is very little writing on the subject of the person of peace. It is also in large part due to the fact that Wolf has taught it so well. Whereas there are hints of the topic mixed in with other people's writing, I am unaware at the time of this writing of any extensive work based on the idea. In fact, a Google search for "Person of Peace" will yield a pdf file of some of Wolf's teaching on the matter as the number one result. Wolf, "Persons of Peace."

gospel message. It also speaks to our need to proclaim the gospel in word and deed on a wide scale, seeing that we are not privy to God's sovereign plan and do not know whom He has called. Again, from Wolf:

> Before you ever make contact, before you ever meet her, before "Peace" is spoken to him, the person of peace has been prepared by God: that person has, within his own life time, among the boundaries of his own life, groped and grappled with self, sin, society, existence, so that the One in whom he lives and continues being has spoken to his inner heart and written codes of truth in such a way that that person, that person of peace, will be born afresh by the word preached. And in the most unpromising of circumstances, wherever there is a person of peace, Christ will enter in.[6]

Jesus couches the teaching in Luke 10 regarding a person of peace in the midst of a much larger story and a great deal more teaching about His mission and how it will be carried out. Two chapters earlier (Luke 8), Jesus tells a story about sowing seed that infers a broad spreading of the seed, not necessarily a particular and painstaking choice about good soil, bad soil, weeds, or other particular dangers that inhibit the gospel's taking root. We see here, again, that we are not privy to who is and who is not called by God and that widespread commendation of the Kingdom is good and necessary.

Following the parable of the sower, however, Jesus speaks about lighting a lamp and not hiding it away, so that whoever enters the home will see it. It is a much more personal approach and one that Jesus echoed as He sent out the 70. Both a widespread witness and personal relationships are important to the spread of the gospel message. The broad witness of the follower of Jesus was important, in part, because it would lead to finding the person of peace.

We are not sent out to find the person of peace. We are sent to proclaim the gospel of the Kingdom. God then uses our proclamation to reveal the persons of peace whom He has prepared beforehand. If our focus becomes finding the person of peace, it may very easily translate into a project of sorts — a selective process of sorting through

---

6 Ibid.

people to find the one. We find in Jesus' directions a command to speak peace and move accordingly as the hearers respond.

Numerous missionaries have embarked on a person of peace "Easter egg hunt" of sorts. They have gone into a new place and bounced from person to person with no concern for relationship, simply asking some church or faith-related question to complete strangers. Asking a teacher in a new place if you can conduct a church function in her school does not equal speaking peace to her, and can sometimes actually be damaging to your reputation and cause.

Our expectation of what it means to be received shapes the way we approach this process. In Luke 9, Jesus sends out the twelve with very similar instructions as in Luke 10. In this passage, however, Jesus tells the disciples to stay where they are received and not stay where they are not received. He does not say anything about the host immediately following Jesus; only that they receive, or welcome, the disciples. If we are welcomed into a place and among a people, it is a strong indication that God is at work there.

Judaism, the religion of the people to whom Christ sent His followers, of course, was well known for its hospitality as commanded in Scriptures (Lev. 19:34, Ex. 12:49), which was well documented throughout Israel's storied history. Abraham eagerly hosted three strangers in Genesis 18; Lot cared for his three visitors in Genesis 19 so vigorously that he offered his two virgin daughters for their protection; Laban hosted a stranger in Genesis 24; David was received and cared for in 2 Samuel 17.27–29; a wealthy couple built on a room for Elisha in 2 Kings 4; and Job wrote that he had been faithful to care for the sojourner in Job 31:32.

Hospitality was a forgone conclusion among the Jews. However, Jesus' followers were preaching something new, a fulfillment of the expectations of the Jews leading to that point. They were preaching the fulfillment of a kingdom for which God's people longed. Some would receive the message, and some would be hostile to it—maybe violently so. It was a frightening endeavor, trusting that their provision would come through the kindness of others. It was also a deeply exciting, encouraging, and faith-building one, knowing that certainly people would respond to the gospel of peace and their needs would be met through their work as ambassadors for Christ's Kingdom.

People, even persons of peace, will respond differently in varying places and cultures. Some may be immediately responsive, like Cornelius in Acts 10. Others may require some persuasion, such as the ones who join Paul and Silas in Acts 17:4. There may be people in certain cultural contexts who move toward faith fairly easily and immediately respond to the Holy Spirit.

On the other hand, there may be those whom God is calling out of a post-Christian or other difficult context who require a bit more relational connection before they open themselves to religious conversation. The simple fact that they are open to relationship with you is cause for celebration, even though the process is slower than with others.

Jesus did not send out the 70 with a mission to find a particular few who would be persons of peace, per se. He had sent them out to represent the Kingdom and proclaim its message, which would inevitably lead them to those whom God had prepared, immediate or not. However, once the person of peace responded, the relationship birthed thereby was leveraged to its fullest, to the extent that he and his household would become the center of the ministry happening in his community.

The person of peace became a sort of to which he belonged. He became a referral for the believer to his friends and family. He became the broker of the currency of relationship. If you look back to Luke 10, you will see that Jesus told the 70 that once the person of peace emerged, they were to move in and receive the hospitality offered them (Luke 10:7–8). They were to basically join his household, at least temporarily; and through the relationship they were to become an acceptable outsider among the people of the community (Luke 10:9).

Finding the person of peace is not a science. It is in its very essence spiritual. When we go, we are not necessarily looking for a person, we are looking for a spirit of peace that resides within a person making that individual open to the gospel. Through the revelation of the person of peace, we are given a divine hint that we are indeed among the people to whom we have been sent and God has prepared the way for a gospel harvest. Our tendency toward the tangible leads us to develop systems, however: The person of peace will have qualities A, B, C, and D. We begin to look for the qualities we have determined to be essential instead of listening to the Spirit and following His leadership to someone who is actually overcome with the Spirit of peace and open to the gospel.

For instance, a common conception of a person of peace is someone who seems relationally well-connected. If someone is going to rely on the relationships of the person of peace for the transmission of the gospel, then he would want to find someone with far-reaching connections. Strangely, though, Jesus commonly called the outcast to Himself. The disciples were not rock stars in their communities. They were physical laborers and not known for their intellect. Matthew was probably hated by most who knew him. Simon was a zealot and likely had plenty of enemies. Jesus even used a demoniac who was living naked, alone, and chained in a graveyard to reach his community.

Here again we see the importance of the Spirit's leadership in mission. We must not rely only on manmade strategies for finding the people with whom we should tie ourselves for the work of ministry. It is the Spirit who called us; it is the Spirit who guides (Gal. 5:25).

### Marks of the Person of Peace

There are three particular marks that characterize the person of peace: receptivity, reputation, and referral.[7]

### 1. Receptivity

The person of peace responds to the gospel (Luke 10:6). As we have previously noted, it may be an immediate or delayed response, but he responds. The book of Acts shows that the response may be through a process of searching the Scriptures, questioning, debating, arguing, dialoguing, and persuading[8]; it may be through an exorcism;[9] or it may even be through a miracle or healing,[10] but response comes. This idea is simple enough, but helps to define the person of peace. He or she is the first within the community or tribe to respond to the gospel and becomes the beginning point or conduit for the rest of the ministry there.

Our natural process of evangelization is to sow first and reap the returns afterward. However, the idea of the person of peace is that God has sovereignly gone before the ones He has sent and prepared the heart already. The seed of the gospel has already been sown (John 4:38). The sent one goes into the harvest not to sow, but to reap the person of peace.

---

7 Ibid.

8 Acts 8:28–35; 17:11–12; 16:31–34; 18:7–8; 17:2–4.

9 Acts 16:6–18.

10 Acts 9:36–43; 14:3–7.

The conversion of Cornelius and his household (Acts 10), the conversion of Lydia and her household (16:14), and the conversion of the Philippian jailer and his household (16:30–33) are all wonderful examples of this idea. These people had their hearts opened by the Lord. God had done the work. The apostles only had to enter the field and reap. The sowing was already done.

Once the person of peace emerged, her *oikos*[11]—or "household," including extended family, friends, and others in the house—was always converted as well, and became an entry point to the rest of the community (e.g., Peter remained with Cornelius working from his home for some days; Lydia opened her home to Paul and Timothy from which they worked in Philippi and through which the Philippian jailer was converted).

In Luke 10:2, Jesus made it clear that "the harvest was plentiful," and there was work to be done. The missing part of the equation was not the ones whom God had sovereignly prepared for response to the gospel; it was those who would work among them. This chapter and this book are certainly not a place to argue the merits of the doctrine of election, but one cannot overlook Jesus' point in the verse: There are those who *will* respond. Influential missiologist Lesslie Newbigin wrote, "From the very beginning God chooses, calls, and sends particular people. God is always the initiator. The words of Jesus to His disciples, 'You did not choose me; I choose you,' are in line with everything in the Bible from beginning to end."[12]

Yet, as we noted earlier in this chapter, those He sent did not know who or where they were, or when they might respond. Jesus' words, then, were meant to be an encouragement for His followers; there would be fruit in their effort. Some people would receive them, thereby receiving Christ (Luke 10:16).

Jesus' words remain a comfort and an encouragement for us and have been across time for those who have been sent in His name. As well, those same words are a challenge to remember that there is work to be done.

---

11 The term *oikos* will be more fully explained in the following chapter, "Engaging Tribes."

12 Newbigin, *The Gospel in a Pluralist Society,* 80.

## Pitfalls

There are a couple of pitfalls to avoid with this idea. The first pitfall lies in the idea that fruitfulness—people responding to the gospel—proves both the call and the faithfulness of the one who is sent. Poor Jeremiah would be crushed if that were so, as would many of the prophets whose words went unheeded by the people to whom they were sent. In one sense that includes Christ Himself, who began His ministry with no one, built it to thousands, maybe even tens of thousands of people, and yet had only 120 gathered in the upper room after He ascended [Acts 1:15].).

To be clear, the work of the follower of Christ is simply obedience – going as Christ has sent him. Drawing men unto Himself is something only God can do (John 6:28–29, 44). Obviously, Jesus expected there would be people who would not receive the gospel; hence His instructions for just such an occurrence in Luke 10:10–11. We only go in obedience to Christ's call; God gives the increase (1 Cor. 3:7).

The second pitfall, closely related to the first, is the mistaken notion that responsiveness dictates our strategy. In other words, we go only where people are visibly responsive to the gospel. That is obviously not what Jesus was telling His followers. He told them they would experience rejection and go to places where people would not respond positively. We should expect some of the same.

As Jesus sends us under the leadership of the Spirit, we are to go to whom He has sent us with the message of good news He has given us regardless of the responsiveness of the people. Matthew Henry wrote of this idea, "They must show, not only their goodwill, but God's good-will, to all to whom they came, and leave the issue and success to him that knows the heart."[13]  Again, people's responses are not our responsibility. Our obedience to Christ's call is. Otherwise, we find ourselves in disobedience and may even miss the opportunity to sow where others may later water and reap (John 4:37; 1 Cor. 3:5–9).

## Sowing

I have tried to make a case for reaping where we have not sown. Clearly, such an argument is warranted, since Jesus said the harvest was

---

13 Henry, "Complete Commentary on the Whole Bible: Luke 10."

plentiful. One does not sow into a harvest; one reaps. For the sake of clarity, though, there is much sowing to be done. I previously made reference to the story of the sower of the seed, which is an example of Christ's teaching on the matter. The existence of a person of peace does not remove from the believer the responsibility of sowing the seed of the gospel; it only offers a platform from which to do so. The person of peace really is a gift. He is a harvest for which we have not worked, but in his company begins the work of sowing inside his relationships (Luke 10:7–9).

## 2. Reputation

The person of peace is not just any convert. Instead, she is a person with a reputation, well-known by those among her family, friends, neighbors, and co-workers—her *oikos* (Luke 10:9). Be careful here, though, because she is not necessarily always a person of good reputation:

Now the person might well be a person of high reputation, as were Cornelius, Lydia, the Ethiopian eunuch, and others. But consider the demon-possessed slave girl with the spirit of divination (Acts 16:16), or the Gerasenes man among the tombs with an unclean spirit. No one was able to bind him anymore. But everyone knew of him. He was a person of reputation, and he manifested himself to be a person of peace.[14]

Missionaries entering a new culture or community often try to begin by finding the people who are "closest" to being Christians. They find the ones who are living by some moral and ethical standards that reflect "goodness." They look for the good people, because it seems they are the easiest ones to help bridge the gap and believe the gospel. That is not always the case. God may call the "worst" among them in order to show His power and glory. In fact, He may cause the foolish to shame the wise (1 Cor. 1:27).

### He Was Demon-Possessed

For instance, take the demon-possessed man in Mark 5. Jesus freed him from torment and changed him. In response, he begged to accompany Jesus but Jesus refused. Instead, he was told to go home and

---

14 "Persons of Peace."

tell his story — all that Jesus had done for him. He did that very thing, and everyone marveled at his words and at who Jesus had made him.

Consider the response of the people of the Decapolis before this man went back home. They had begged Jesus to leave the area (Mark 5:17). They literally begged Him to go. However, after the man went back to his town (having been a man of horrible reputation changed by Jesus), shared with them all that Christ had done, and lived among them, the response of the people to Jesus changed. They were not just open to Him, but pleading for Him to work among them.

In Mark 7.31, Jesus returned to the Decapolis. The people there, the same ones who had previously begged Him to leave, began to beg Him to heal a deaf man in their community. They wanted Him there. They had heard from the person of peace of the goodness and mercy of Jesus. They had seen it clearly in a manner they understood. A man of their community, one everyone all knew and feared, was once again in his right mind and living among them. They understood because of his story. He had received the gospel, and his community was changed along with him.

### They Are "Bad" People

Think of the modern tribes that are influenced by a rock star, athlete, or actor who has a horrible reputation as a womanizer, addict, and partier. Suddenly, Jesus grapples with this person's soul and everything changes. The people see the drastic change in who he is. Because of the change they see in him, those within his tribe also begin to wrestle with truth. Saul's conversion is the perfect example of this type of influence found in Acts 9:20–22:

> 20 And immediately he proclaimed Jesus in the synagogues, saying, "He is the Son of God." 21 And all who heard him were amazed and said, "Is not this the man who made havoc in Jerusalem of those who called upon this name? And has he not come here for this purpose, to bring them bound before the chief priests?" 22 But Saul increased all the more in strength, and confounded the Jews who lived in Damascus by proving that Jesus was the Christ.

Saul experienced Jesus on the road to Damascus, and his eyes were opened to see who Jesus was. Saul's reputation preceded him, making Ananias afraid to talk to him as he was commanded in a vision (Acts

9:11–16) and causing amazement among the Jews who heard him preaching Jesus.

### They Are "Good" People

Numerous examples exist of the *oikos* of an individual being changed because of his or her good reputation. Cornelius, Lydia, and the Philippian jailer were all highly esteemed among their people, who were converted right along with them.[15]

This is the effect of the person of peace. It works on a smaller scale as well, and not just with rock stars and people of poor reputation. I currently have no influence among the local DJ scene in the city where I live. It is not a very large tribe, but none of them know me. Therefore, they have no reason to listen to me or trust what I have to say.

Things would change if I could befriend one among them, reap where God has already sown, and leverage my relationship with this new person of peace to gain credibility with his friends. His reputation among his friends is the currency for gaining an audience with his tribe.

## 3. Referral

The person of peace refers the gospel through influence via existing relationships (Luke 10:7–9). As we have seen in the previous examples, these relationships are a conduit for mission. As we "take up residence" with them and work from their vantage point, we gain an audience with whomever they already had an audience.

To help understand referral, we can examine the communal nature of fish. All fish school, and they are led as they swim by what scientists call the fish of reference. Those fish initiate every turn within the school. It turns and the others follow.

Just as the school of fish needs one to turn first so that others can follow, groups of people, or tribes, also need someone to lead out by turning first.[16] An outsider seldom turns an entire tribe. His best hope is to become an acceptable outsider who is brought into the tribe through relationship with the person of peace. This person of peace then, is of utmost importance to the missionary as she builds new

---

15 Acts 10; 16:14–15, 25–34.

16 "Persons of Peace."

relationships and takes the gospel to new people and places, whether in her own home town or around the globe.[17]

## Posture

As we live on mission and enter new relationships, our posture is important. The manner in which we approach people often determines the manner in which they respond. The concept of the person of peace requires a certain posture, one of humility and vulnerability.

Jesus commanded His followers to go into the harvest without much provision, leaving them fully dependent on the people to whom they were sent. He also warned them they would face rejection. They could not take it personally. Both of these aspects of their being sent out required them to lay down pride and self-dependence and approach the people to whom they were sent in humility and thankfulness.

Mission is often portrayed as one person who has something that another person needs offering it to him as a solution to his "problem" and a means to garner an audience for gospel proclamation. This is not inherently a bad thing. The problem comes in the posture of the missionary and has everything to do with pride.

I know of an American church that felt called to work in a particular area of Spain. They decided their point of entry into the culture would be through hosting soccer camps for children. Of course, soccer is immensely important in Spain. There are real soccer players there. Every kid in Spain grows up playing the game and playing it well. Even so, this group coming from the United States where soccer is not all that big a deal, wanted to teach Spanish children to play the game they already loved.

A wise missionary counseled the church instead to join a Spanish-led soccer camp and learn from them. Changing the way they chose to approach the people would change their posture. Instead of coming in with all the answers which would have very likely turned off the Spanish people they hoped to know, he encouraged the church group to lower its posture, which would likely lower the guard of the people

---

17 By "missionary," I mean to say Christian, not just full-time Christian worker. All followers of Christ are meant to join Him on mission (Matt. 28:18–20; Acts 1:8, et al.), thereby making them missionaries. This tool is important for an American marketplace worker in Europe, a full-time Chinese Christian worker in the Middle East, and someone living on mission in the same city where he grew up.

from whom they were learning. They would move from a perceived air of pride as the teachers to humility as learners.

Jesus chose to come in this way. Paul wrote of Jesus in Philippians 2 that "He made himself nothing," and He "humbled Himself to the point of death, even death on a cross." Christ came in the most humble form He could have, as a baby, with no way to fend for Himself and completely dependent on the hospitality of the ones to whom He came for His survival. Some accepted him well, while others did not.

Christ's humility was not an accident but a purposeful choice, and one that He taught His followers to make as well:

- "I did not come to be served, but to serve" (Matt. 20:28).
- "The first shall be last, and the last shall be first" (Matt. 20:16).
- "Whoever would be great among you must be your servant" (Matt. 20:26).
- "Whoever would be first must be your slave" (Matt. 20:27).
- "Take up your cross and follow me" (Matt. 16:24).
- "Who is the greatest, you ask? Humble yourself like a child" (Matt. 18:1–4).

In Luke 10:3–16, Jesus again asked His followers to do the same, to become subservient and lower themselves to be dependent on those to whom they were sent. Approaching people this way would make it easier to combat their natural sinful pride. Jesus gave His followers a continual reminder to constantly bear their cross well and walk in humility. The good news they offered was the same good news offered them by Christ; and it was not of themselves, it was the free gift of God, not of works, lest they (we) should boast (Eph. 2:8).

We must be careful how we approach others as we follow Jesus on mission. The way we approach them often determines the way they react. If we are to find the person of peace, we must approach him humbly as Christ demonstrated for us.

**Person of Goodwill**

Pertinent to the conversation is another idea about a person who can be quite helpful as we go on mission. He is commonly called the person of goodwill. We see several instances of the person of goodwill in Scripture although this title is never stated.

A person of goodwill is one who shows the follower of Christ kindness along the journey, because God has turned his heart toward the missionary. It may even be only for a little while. The differentiating characteristic between the person of peace and the person of goodwill is the transformational change in their lives. The person of peace changes from one who does not follow Jesus into one who does. That is not the case for the person of goodwill.

Throughout Scripture, moments exist in which God used non-believers to serve His people in their mission with no indication that they became believers themselves. In Ezra 1:2–4, Cyrus, the pagan king of Persia, made a proclamation that God had charged him to build a temple for Him in Jerusalem. He sent all of the Israelites within his kingdom back to Jerusalem and instructed his own people to give them silver and gold, animals and other goods, and anything else they might need for the temple. Cyrus even returned everything Nebuchadnezzar had taken from the temple when Jerusalem had been conquered by Babylon. No indication was made that Cyrus then followed God. He was simply a vessel of goodwill for God's people. God used a non-believer to accomplish the thing He desired.

In Ezra 6 and 7, Persian King Darius made a decree that God's people be able to continue the work of building the temple, and Persian King Artaxerxes sent Ezra out with his authority to take God's people, go to Jerusalem to set up a system of government and live, and take provision from his people along the way. Ezra worshiped the Lord for turning the heart of the pagan king:

> 27 Blessed be the LORD, the God of our fathers, who put such a thing as this into the heart of the king, to beautify the house of the LORD that is in Jerusalem, 28 and who extended to me his steadfast love before the king and his counselors, and before all the king's mighty officers. I took courage, for the hand of the LORD my God was on me, and I gathered leading men from Israel to go up with me.

Artaxerxes' heart was also turned toward Nehemiah who asked the king not only to allow him to go and rebuild the temple, but also to ensure safe passage and provide the materials for the project (Neh. 2:1–8)! The hand of the Lord was certainly on Nehemiah (Neh. 2:8), and He continually used unbelievers to enable His people to obey His commands.

The person of goodwill can be an invaluable resource for the modern missionary as well. He may come in the form of

- a non-believing business owner who knowingly allows believers to meet in his place of business;
- an unbelieving immigrations officer who helps a missionary figure out how to stay in the country and what paper work needs to be filled out to do so;
- a border control agent who searches a missionary's bags and somehow doesn't notice the suitcase full of Bibles in the van;
- a political leader who suddenly, and maybe momentarily, loosens control of the people who can legally enter the country.

Luba was a student at a prestigious university in Moscow. She held to Russian Orthodox beliefs but did not have a personal relationship with Jesus. When a missionary family moved into the area, they were constantly asked if she was a part of their efforts to engage university students. After meeting her, they found she became a magnet for their work among students, constantly referring peers, friends, and relatives to be in relationship with them. Throughout the missionaries' time in Moscow, Luba never showed any interest in pursuing anything more than her Orthodox practices, and she likely never knew the impact she had for the Kingdom in building all of the relational connections for the missionaries. She had no idea she was a person of goodwill being used by the Lord for His purposes.

The person of goodwill is certainly important in fulfilling God's mission, but should not be confused with the person of peace. Notice that neither Ezra nor Nehemiah tried to convince the kings who helped them that they should follow God. They simply recognized that it was God's hand that had turned the hearts of the kings (Prov. 21:1), and they continued on mission.

Our tendency may be to try to find the border control or customs agent after our encounter with them and share the gospel. If led by the Spirit to do so, then certainly sharing with them is the right thing to do. However, it may be that God is simply directing the agent according to His will for our good and His purposes. These people may never follow God or even recognize the role they have played in advancing His mission.

Isaiah prophesied Cyrus would be the king who would deliver God's people from the Babylonian captivity long before his actual rise to the throne of Persia. In doing so, Isaiah called Cyrus the anointed of the Lord (Isa. 45:1). God said Cyrus was His shepherd who would fulfill His purposes (Isa. 44:28). The Israelites recognized that God was at work and moved on to rebuild Jerusalem and the Temple as God had commanded. They did not return to Cyrus to convince him to follow the one true God, and there is no indication that he ever did.

So it is with the person of goodwill. He may never follow God, but thankfully, God still uses him for His purposes and for our good.

## WHAT NOW?: HOW-TO

We have seen the principle of the person of peace in Scripture, but the specifics of its application are less clear.

First, foremost, and continually—pray (1 Thess. 5:17). Jesus directs His followers to do so as He sends them into the harvest (Luke 10:2). He tells them to ask the Lord to send laborers into the harvest. It is God who sends people out. It is also God who determines when and how they go. I will not belabor this point, because there is much more on it in the chapter on being Spirit-led; but central to the principle of the person of peace, as with every aspect of Christian life and mission, is prayer.

Finding the people God has appointed and prepared to receive the gospel and its messengers is not an easy task. A systematic approach to finding persons of peace usually does not yield results. Therefore, our approach must be less "strategic" and more spiritual in nature.

Again, we do not know the ones God has prepared for our coming but we trust that He does. We must follow the encouragement we find in Scripture to simply ask God, who responds when we ask.[18] He will lead us as we pray and he will speak for us as we go (Luke 21:14–15).

Secondly, after we pray or as we continually pray, we move among the relationships God births. As He leads us to a person of peace, we are to dwell with him. This does not necessarily mean moving into the garage apartment. It means living life together, knowing who they know, and working within the existing relational structures around them.

In providing us with persons of peace, God is clearing the way for a relational transfer of the gospel along pre-existing lines. If we do not use the relationships He gives us through the persons of peace, we will

---

18  1 John 3:22; Matthew 7:7–8; James 1:5.

be blazing a new trail when He has already cleared one for us. These people are clear paths to the relationships around them; therefore, we dwell with them and enjoy the gift of God by which the gospel finds its way into new communities.

Thirdly, we must know when it is time to move on. Just as Jesus prescribed the method by which His followers would enter a town and stay when received, he also prescribed how they would leave a town that rejected them (Luke 10:10–15). They would certainly face rejection, trouble, and danger (John 16:33; 17:14). The real question dealt not with if they would struggle but how they would handle struggles when they came. Would they be personally offended and angered because they were rejected?

To teach them how they should respond in this situation, Jesus reminded His followers they were not actually the ones people would be rejecting. They would be ambassadors sent to the people in someone else's name. People's rejection would not be of the sent ones, but of the sender, the One in whose name they would come. The people would actually be rejecting God.

"The one who hears you hears me, and the one who rejects you rejects me, and the one who rejects me rejects the One who sent me" (Luke 10:16). The punishment fits the crime. Reject God, and He rejects you and judgment will be hell. Jesus' admonition is to either find the person of peace and dwell with him, or to recognize decisive rejection and move on (e.g. Acts 13:51; 17:1–14; 18:4–11).

Nevertheless, we need to be very careful when it comes to moving on. I do not read in Luke 10 that we should make a quick gospel presentation, listen for a response, and move on if the hearer does not immediately come to faith. In fact, in reading the Book of Acts, we see the early church being soundly rejected, imprisoned, beaten, and stoned, only to return right back to the same city to continue preaching the same gospel[19]. Apparently, the early Church did not see those moments as decisive rejection, because they returned to the places and people who mistreated them.

On the other hand, we also see situations in which moving on was the necessary choice. One such occasion occurred in Antioch in Pisidia and is found in Acts 13. Paul boldly preaches the gospel in the synagogue on the Sabbath and many Jews respond. They beg Paul and

---

19 Acts 4:3, 18–21; 5:17–21, 40–42; 14:19–21, et al.

Barnabas to return the next week, which they do, and most of the city shows up to hear the gospel.

Some of the Jews began to argue with them, so Paul turned his attention to the Gentiles and many believed. Even so, the Jews and other officials drove Paul and Barnabas out of the city. Acts 13:51 recorded that Paul and Barnabas "shook off the dust from their feet against them." There was successful work within the city. People believed and yet Paul and Barnabas moved on. Neither of these situations seems to jive with Jesus' instruction to stay where we are received and shake off the dust from our feet when we are not, so there must be a spiritual element to the process.

The disciples received the Holy Spirit, and it was the Spirit, whom Jesus had sent who was leading them, telling them where and when to go or not to go (Acts 13:2; 16:6–10; 18:9–11, et al). In the same way, the Spirit leads us as we go. Many people prefer black-and-white strategies. The tension of operating inside the gray is difficult. It would be easiest to have a very clear if/then chart for when and where to go on mission, but that would lessen the importance of knowing and hearing God.

Certainly, Jesus gave us a strategy—go where we are welcomed and leave where we are not. The difficult part is we may not always know exactly what it means to be welcomed or exactly when we are being rejected. The lesson we must learn here is that planning and strategy are important and excellent tools as we go. However, we must hold loosely to our plans and strategies in favor of the leadership of our Lord. It is He who will lead us down the natural avenue for taking the gospel to a new culture; the person of peace, and it is He who will lead us away to the next one.

# ENGAGING TRIBES

[chapter 7]

BY CALEB CRIDER

Growing up in a California suburb, our social lines were not drawn according to ethnicity or economics. Our social groups were the stereotypical cliques: the jocks, the preps, the geeks, the punks, the cowboys, and the surfers (after all, this was California). Every clique had its own place on campus at lunch. Each group had its own style, hangouts, and its own language. My life was a John Hughes movie.

Schoolyard cliques fell into broader categories as well. The popular kids were always the jocks and surfers, while the geeks and Christians were lumped into the non-cool category. Yes, we church kids had our own clique. We were lucky if the jocks even knew who we were. The only way a Christian kid was ever going to be considered cool was if he could become a jock.

If you took the term literally, a jock would have been anyone who participated in a sport. Certainly making the team was one step toward entry into the club, but lots of guys on the team still had to sit with the non-cool kids at lunch. Being a jock meant much more than just being an athlete.

A jock wore baseball hats and varsity letter jackets to let everyone know his status. He referred to professional football players by their last names only, and could cite sports statistics that he heard watching ESPN Sports Center© instead of doing his homework. He was a tough guy, the kind who got in fights and could grow a beard. A jock usually had a girlfriend on his arm, a muscle car in his driveway, and no time for geeks and losers. It meant something to be a jock, and he worked hard to belong to the group.

In high school, we called them "cliques." Missiologists call them "tribes."

Perhaps the single most significant observation in missions today is this — people everywhere are tribal. For most of us, the word "tribe" brings to mind a primitive group of hunters and gatherers living in thatched-roof huts. In this sense, a tribe is a clan, a sort of extended family a person is born into.

Humans are social beings. Theologian and professor Stanley Grenz wrote that humankind was created for community.[1] We relate to society by attaching ourselves relationally to certain people. These groups provide us with a sense of identity; they give us a sense of who we are in relation to others. The group provides things like protection and support while asking for the same in return. Humans languish in

---

1 Grenz, *Created for Community*, 79.

isolation. Apart from our social circles, we tend to lose our sense of who we are.

In his textbook on cross-cultural communication, missiologist David Hesselgrave pointed out that in times past, the barriers that separated people were mainly physical—great distances, mountains, seas, and the like.[2] Urbanization, however, is changing that.

As of 2008, more than half the world's population lived in urban centers.[3] As humanity has moved into cities, we've largely left the family structures we were born into. Many reasons exist for this change. The city provides opportunity unavailable in rural areas. Educated people rarely return to the small towns they came from to work on the family farm. Tiny downtown apartments just don't have the room for an extended family to all live together, and the cost of living in the city can be quite expensive. Consequently, family is quickly losing its place as the center of our social lives.

City dwellers haven't ceased to be tribal, they've just adapted to their urban reality. French sociologist Michel Maffesoli introduced the idea of the urban tribe in 1985.[4] His research into neo-tribalism showed that while rural social groupings tend to be driven by authoritative systems of power, urban dwellers are socially motivated by peer influence and energy. Rather than being organized around family, modern tribes are voluntary and tend to be based on affinity. People select their social circles, however subconsciously, to replace the clans they were born into but serve the same functions.

Consider the gangs of homeless children in the slums of India. They band together to survive the streets by looking out for one another and sharing what they have. For many young African men, the ranks of regional militias provide the father figures and familial structure they would never otherwise have known. Upwardly mobile adult children of divorced parents form social circles that serve as group therapy. Blue-collar workers who routinely put their lives in the hands of coworkers form a bond that is stronger than blood relations. Around the world, and at every level, humans are increasingly tribal.

---

2 Hesselgrave, *Communicating Christ Cross-Culturally*, 96.

3 United Nations Population Fund, "Introduction."

4 Maffesoli, *The Time of the Tribes*, 72.

## Modern Tribes

No matter the context, tribes are the social circles we move in. A tribe is the primary social unit to which a person may belong. A tribe has rules, structure, leadership, and goals. Modern tribes may range in connectedness from tightly- to loosely-knit, and people respond differently to each. Tribes are complex structures.

Tribes are where people gain their sense of identity. As social beings, we define ourselves by the company we keep (or, more specifically, the company we want to keep). It means something to be a member of a particular tribe; who we are and who we are not. In his book, Tribes, Seth Godin explains that a tribe is any group of people who are connected to one another, a leader, and an idea.[5]

Some examples of tribes:

• Massai of Kenya and Tanzania
• Navajo of North America
• The Wolof of Senegal
• High school cliques
• Apple Macintosh computer users
• Rush Limbaugh listeners
• The Catholic Church

A person may belong to one or several social groupings, but any may serve as an individual's public self-identification. All tribes have common characteristics.

Just as a fraternity or sorority has a period of initiation for potential members, tribes have rites of passage that clearly define who is "in" and who is "out." A loosely-knit tribe may have low barriers for entry — to be a Mac user, one needs only to purchase a MacBook. Joining the Marines, on the other hand, requires basic training and a four-year commitment. While membership of most tribes is open, some require insider approval for admittance.

Because tribes are social structures, each has its own rules. Norms for acceptable behavior may not be explicitly stated, but are understood by insiders. A tribe may have rules about courting and marriage, gender roles, or politics. Members of some tribes are forbidden from socializing

---

5 Godin, *Tribes*, 1.

with another tribe. Most tribes even have members who serve to enforce the tribe's rules.

The problem with being an outsider desiring to affect change on the inside is that as an outsider, you don't usually know the rules. Because most tribes don't greet you with an orientation packet, you're in a race to learn the rules before you break them all. There are always consequences for breaking a tribe's rules ranging from embarrassment to excommunication or worse.

Tribe members have an insider language. For isolated or closed tribes, this will be an actual language. Among tribes that are more open, insider-speak is comprised of a common vocabulary that reflects the worldview of the group. For example, many younger groups have adopted sarcasm as their primary means of expression. The uninitiated may mistake a sarcastic vote of approval as authentic. Insiders, on the other hand, understand that what is said isn't always what's meant.

Other examples of tribal languages can be found in the United States among politically conservative radio talk show hosts. Despite the fact that he doesn't actually know every member of his audience, Sean Hannity greets his callers with "You're a Great American!" Rush Limbaugh's diehard fans (called "ditto-heads") wish the host "mega-dittos" as an affirmation of his ideology. The broader conservative audience uses words like *conservative, liberal, government, and socialist* but defines them differently than those on the other side of the political spectrum who have their own insider-speak.

The implications of insider language to mission are great. If mission is overcoming barriers to the spread of the gospel through incarnation, language is among the most difficult to overcome. In order to translate the gospel across cultures, we must take into account every tribe's unique patterns of communication. The missionary may find that he needs to rely on a specific mode of communication for each group. Older people may need direct personal interaction while tech-connected younger tribes may prefer highly-abbreviated text messaging. The gospel will not be spread where it is not appropriately communicated.

Tribes also typically wear uniforms. The stereotypes reveal the importance of appearance: the Maasai wear red striped sarongs, hippies wear their hair long, and Rastafarians sport dreadlocks. Country folk wear camouflage, city boys tote messenger bags. Hipsters these days wear vintage plaid flannel over their tattoos, while steampunks show off their self-designed modified retro-future Victorian apparel. Soccer moms shop at Old Navy. Physical appearance is a social cue that helps people express their tribal identity and recognize the affiliations of others. To an outsider, members of a group may all seem to dress alike; but insiders recognize uniforms that advertise status. High-power business people wear nicer suits. Rappers wear jewelry to signify their success. Cowboys can spot high-dollar boots from a mile away. No self-respecting freegan would be caught dead in firsthand clothing. The school yard is divided by knockoff sneakers.

Whether formal or informal, all tribes have some form of leadership. Some tribes are built around a single personality, while others may look to a core group of founders for guidance or inspiration. Others still may have unknown leaders who prefer to remain behind the scenes. Without leadership, tribes tend to stall, fragment, or disintegrate altogether.

Tribal leadership can take many different approaches. Some tribes elect leaders. Others follow whomever they deem to be the greatest among them. Consider the culinary world: Outsiders may care about Cooking Channel reality show hosts, but insiders follow the examples of those who are named "great" by the industry. Michelin Stars, James Beard awards, and successful restaurants mean added influence for a chef.

### The Search to Belong

In his 2003 book, *The Search to Belong*, Joseph Myers outlined four major levels of belonging that all people seek—public, social, personal, and intimate.[6] These spaces, as Myers calls them, meet key needs in our lives. The public space is an open and broad social affiliation like being a fan of a particular sports team or driving a certain model of car. The social space fills a more specific need for meaningful interaction, such as one might have gotten in times past from talking to neighbors while sitting on the front porch. Myers' concept of personal space is where the private interaction occurs — things like sharing personal problems or asking for advice. The last space, the intimate, says Myers, is reserved for one or two people with whom we have uninhibited, completely open and honest relationships.

The four spaces are a great way to understand the tribes from a missiological perspective. At one time, all four spaces were filled by

---

6 Myers, *The Search to Belong*, 20.

family. Today, people choose their communities to meet their needs. Sports teams, clubs, churches, and political parties all serve a social function for their fans and members.

When I was a child, my family moved from Southern California to the San Francisco Bay area. The four-hundred-mile move north was a radical change for us: we left the laid-back, diverse, and warm Los Angeles urban sprawl for San Francisco's uptight, uniform, and colder climate. For as long as I could remember, we had been fans of the Los Angeles Dodgers baseball team. Some of my best memories were of outings to games at the hilltop stadium near downtown Los Angeles.

Now, we had moved to the territory of the Dodgers' arch-rivals — the San Francisco Giants. My dad and I knew that our Dodger blue hats and shirts wouldn't be welcome here, so we made a conscious decision to adjust our loyalties. To mark the occasion, we held a little ceremony. Dad got tickets to the season opener at Candlestick Park, the (then) Giants stadium. We put away our Dodgers' T-shirts for good, went to the game, bought Giants hats, and cheered for the home team. Just like that, we were Giants fans.

Maybe we weren't the best fans. Perhaps we should have stayed true to our team even after the move. We certainly weren't excited about switching teams. But something about attending that game and buying those hats made the San Francisco Bay area home for me. It was as if, simply by wearing the right colors, we had camouflaged ourselves as locals. At school and in the neighborhood, I didn't stand out quite as much as I had before. Our whole family had started to refer to the collective "we" that sports fans do, as in, "We had a great win last night against Atlanta. Hope we can sweep the next three against the Cubs." Becoming Giants fans meant we settled in and identified with our new community.

To say that people "choose" their community is not to say they are happy with the community they have. Sometimes, people become stuck in a social circle that doesn't meet their needs. This is the problem with most existing social structures; they fail to live up to the needs and expectations of their members.

Furthermore, to say that people select their tribes based on affinity doesn't mean they are any less influential than clan-based tribes. Actually, these chosen social circles often have more influence on the individual simply because the act of choosing them reflects on the one doing the choosing. A person doesn't have any say in what family he's born into, but selecting a social group and going to the trouble of joining it means having much more invested in the resulting connections.

## The Function of a Tribe

Tribes do more than just provide their members with a sense of identity. They help the individual process new information. Every day people are bombarded with information. The tribe serves as a filter through which to process that information. Members may discover something new like information about an upcoming event or insight into a social event. Then they bring that new information to the group, sharing what they've learned (thereby informing everyone else) and essentially asking, "What do we believe about this?" The underlying question each member is asking is, "What do I believe about this?" The tribe's response will then determine what the individual does with this newly discovered information.

A good example can be found online. Social media provide users with virtual connections and a constant stream of (mostly trivial) data. Every time someone uploads a link to a particularly clever political cartoon or a video of a cat that has learned to knit, he is basically thinking, "I found this and thought it might be of interest to the tribe." When the tribe likes the link, the user is encouraged to find more such information. But a negative response (or no response at all) from one's peers communicates, "This isn't important to us."

Many missionaries employ a methodology that relies strictly on a one-to-one proclamation of the gospel. The thinking, of course, is that a decision to follow Christ is personal and individual. However, as tribally-connected people, we are limited in our capacity to process major life decisions on our own. Tribal people do much of their thinking in community.

## Narrative

In the past, information was hard to come by. People relied on newspapers and marketplace gossip for information about the world. With knowledge came power, whoever controlled the flow of information controlled society. When information is scarce, it is valuable. That's why our grandparents spent hundreds of dollars on twenty-volume sets of encyclopedias for their homes. Finding information was a chore. Not long ago, doing research meant wading through card catalogs and microfiche.

Times have changed. With the advent of the Internet, we moved from a dearth of information to open access to unlimited amounts of information in a relatively short period of time. For the first time in history, information is constant. We are truly overwhelmed with information from the web, text messages, TV, radio, cell phones, and print.

Every day we're bombarded with noise. Buy this car! Eat that cereal! Beware of the danger lurking just beneath the surface of your kitchen cutting board! Everywhere we go someone wants our time, money, and loyalty. The American Marketing Association defines an advertisement as: "Any announcement or persuasive message placed in the mass media in paid or donated time or space by an identified individual, company, or organization." According to that definition, the average person living in a major city is exposed to as many as 5,000 advertisements per day![7]

What people need now isn't more information, but filters to sort through the information they already have access to. Good information versus bad; helpful versus hurtful.

Rather than sort through information on our own, people seek influential narrators who filter through the data and offer a complete perspective. The world is then viewed through the narrative lens of people like news commentators, celebrities, authors, radio hosts, religious leaders, politicians, and story-tellers. Some tribes have local narrators, while others rely on gatekeepers who manage the flow of information into the group.

Television hosts can be especially influential narrators. Every day for 25 years, millions of Americans tuned into the Oprah Winfrey Show, a lifestyle television talk show, to hear Oprah talk about life from her perspective. Through interviews, Oprah brought out the humanity in personal stories that allowed her viewers to make emotional connections. The show discussed everything under the sun, from relationships to household organization to health and well-being to book recommendations. Oprah was a narrator. People across the country depended on her to define what should be important for them and to demonstrate how they should feel about those things.

---

7 Story, "Anywhere the Eye Can See, It's Likely to See an Ad."

Narratives most often include major perspectives, meta-themes such as what is wrong with the world, who is the enemy, what would make the world better, and what are preferred solutions. This includes elements that address: How does the world view me, and what are my values and priorities? A narrative is a story that explains a tribe's place in the world.

It's important to understand the narrative of the people to whom you minister. It's the worldview language they speak. Tribes are formed around these narratives. Here you find the questions the gospel directly addresses: What binds the people? What motivates them? Who among them is hurting? What spiritual influences are evident?

## Churches Waiting to Happen

It might be tempting to see tribes as barriers to the spread of the gospel. After all, if every social group has its own narrative and requires a unique approach to incarnation, we clearly don't have enough missionaries to make a difference. But viewed another way, tribes are very good for mission. These are essentially groups who meet regularly, enjoy fellowship, tell stories, counsel, support, serve one another, and provide members with a sense of identity. These characteristics may sound familiar because they are the same sorts of things we'd expect to see in a local church.[8]

Of course, unless the members of the group know Christ and meet together for His glory, a tribe is not a church, not yet anyway. But among many tribes, the infrastructure is there, already established, but waiting to be jumpstarted to life by the Holy Spirit. Most of the work of church planting is already done for us — tribes are churches waiting to happen!

Because tribes are potential churches, the common missionary behavior of extraction needs to be questioned. Extraction, according to missional thinker Alan Hirsch, is a typical method of discipleship that removes a new believer from his existing social surroundings in order to acculturate him into an established church.[9] For example, a missionary

---

8 "A local church is a group of professing believers who meet regularly for worship, prayer, to study the scriptures, and fellowship. Members of the church minister to one another's needs, hold each other accountable, and exercise church discipline as needed. Members encourage one another and build each other up in holiness, maturity in Christ, and love." International Mission Board, "Definition Of Church."

9 Hirsch and Ford, *Right Here Right Now*, 215.

is necessarily an outsider when it comes to tribes of unbelievers. As an outsider, he shares the gospel indiscriminately, and by God's grace, some are saved. This, of course, is a very good thing. But the next step is vital. Most missionaries gather those who have come to faith into a new group and consider it a new church. The missionary then switches from evangelism mode to discipleship mode and begins to teach the group of new believers how to do church. Before long, this group of people needs to be encouraged to go out and make non-Christian friends. Churches hold seminars and training sessions about how to relate to lost people. The result is a synthetic, manufactured, Christian tribe that mimics the world's tribes. We end up with a Christian clique just as closed and exclusive as the other groups.

In the short run, this approach may be effective because it results in a new gathering of Christians. It makes sense that we would want to remove a new believer from the negative influences of his pagan social environment in order to teach him. But if we were to take a step back and consider the tribes in which people live, we would see that extraction is extremely destructive of the very relational channels along which the gospel would spread.

Rather than seeing the process of conversion to life in Christ, other tribe members only see their fellow tribesmen whisked away by an outsider who proceeds to indoctrinate them into a foreign religion and culture. Extraction divides, isolates, and confuses. Instead of encouraging the tribe to consider as a group the implications of the gospel for their lives, it forces them to process the good news as individuals– something they're not equipped to do. Because people are tribal, we shouldn't be in such a rush to plug everyone into a church. In doing so, we build forced, awkward groups with little influence on one another. These new Christian relationships begin to negatively replace the natural ones.

What if, instead of seeing existing social structures as barriers to the spread of the good news, we began to see them as direct lines of communication? Instead of considering every person as an individual, we could consider them as representatives of a tribe. In this light, the gospel is boldly proclaimed into a social circle, and entire groups are discipled. The gospel is trusted to permeate the tribe's discussion and haunt its members' interactions with one another. The resulting group can then take charge of communicating the good news within the tribe. They can demonstrate for others what life in Christ truly means for people of their kind.

## Spiritual Life Support

Being slow to extract people from their social circles does have serious implications for their spiritual formation. Surrounded by influences that are less than God-honoring, a new disciple may struggle to break out of his former mindset. It's much more difficult to "take off the old man and put on the new" when everyone around is quite happy with the old man. The possibility exists that a person left in his social environment would have to wait a very long time for Christian community among his own tribe. Discipleship seems much more efficient in an environment we control.

It may take a long time for a tribe to come to faith. In the meantime, we can serve as the *spiritual life-support* for the individual(s) who believe by encouraging, teaching, and praying until the body comes to life.

The value of discipling someone in place is tremendous. New believers learn to apply their faith to real life, a process that results in indigenous expressions of church. Their theology is done in their own language, and their missionary identity is sealed into their DNA. We end up with a Christianized tribe who is equipped for the task of cultural translation of the gospel. They can relate without having to learn a new language or social rules.

## Tribes in the New Testament

What about Jesus? Didn't He extract the disciples from their secular lives when He called on them to drop their nets and follow Him? Well, yes and no. Certainly the gospel is a call to complete and utter abandonment of life as we know it. Following Jesus doesn't necessarily mean that we leave behind the allegiances and identities of our previous life (Matt. 10:37). But it doesn't mean that we must disconnect from the tribes we were in when the gospel found us. The twelve disciples left everything to follow Jesus, but they followed Him in and around their hometowns in full view of their peers.

Throughout the New Testament, tribes are significant in the spread of the gospel. Upon meeting Jesus, Andrew ran to his brother Simon (Peter) saying, "We have found the Messiah!" (John 1:40–42). Likewise, Philip took the news of Jesus to Nathaniel, proclaiming, "We have found the one Moses wrote about in the Law, and about whom the prophets also wrote — Jesus of Nazareth, the son of Joseph" (John

1:44-45). In His Revelation, God casts a vision for every "tribe, tongue, and nation" before His throne at the end of time.[10]

Modern translations of the Scriptures don't actually use the word "tribes" to refer to these social groupings. In the Ancient Greek, the word *oikos* is translated "household" but carries the same meaning as "tribe." The Greek concept of household would have meant much more than just the structure, building, or even nuclear family. The household was everyone who pertained to a person's societal group—family, extended family, employees, servants—anyone who shared an interdependent life together.

In his paper, *Oikos Evangelism: The Biblical Pattern*, sociologist Thom Wolf wrote about the importance of the tribe to first-century thinking[11]: "An *oikos* was the fundamental and natural unit of society, and consisted of one's sphere of influence — his family, friends, and associates. And equally important, the early church spread through "oikoses" — circles of influence and association."

1. When we read about Zacchaeus in Luke 19, we see Jesus inviting Himself over to dinner at the tax collector's house (a terrific missional strategy), and teaching Zacchaeus's groups of friends. Jesus departs saying, "Today salvation has come to this household" (*oikos*, Luke 19:9).

2. After Levi left everything and followed Jesus, the tax collector held a great banquet for Jesus at his house, and invited his tax collector friends (Luke 5:27–32).

3. An angel instructed Cornelius to seek out Peter in order to hear a message "by which he would be saved, and his entire household" (*oikos*, Acts 11:14).

4. In Philippi, God opened Lydia's heart to the gospel and, according to the Scriptures "she was baptized, with her household" (*oikos*, Acts 16:15).

5. Also in Philippi, Paul declared to the Philippian Jailer, "Believe in the Lord Jesus Christ, and you will be saved, you and your

---

10 Revelation 5:9–10; 7:9,14; 13:6–7; 14:6–7.

11 Wolf, "Oikos Evangelism."

household." Then they spoke the word of the Lord to him and to all that were in his *oikos*, and the result was that "he rejoiced with all his household that he had believed in God" (Acts 16:31).

6. Later in Acts, we read that Crispus, the ruler of the synagogue in Corinth "believed in the Lord, together with all his household" (Acts 18:8). Paul demonstrates the importance of *oikos* to his ministry when he writes about baptizing Crispus and the household of Stephanas in 1 Corinthians 1:14–16.

The word *oikos* is mentioned so often in the Scriptures that we can see a pattern; not only individuals repenting and following Jesus, but entire households. It's not entirely clear how this happened. Perhaps the leader of each *oikos* held such influence that the rest of the members naturally followed suit and converted. Or maybe it was the power of seeing one of theirs respond so radically to Christ. The fact that Paul was willing to baptize the various members of each *oikos* makes it clear that the belief of the tribe was simultaneous and genuine.

## An Outsider's Influence

The question arises: Are we, as missionaries at home or abroad, supposed to try to join a tribe in order to influence it, create a new one altogether, or can we remain outsiders, preach the gospel, and expect to see tribes come to faith? The answer depends on the leadership of the Holy Spirit. Some missionaries are compelled by the urgency of the mission to conform to a culture only insofar as it allows them to proclaim the gospel. Others are inspired to immerse themselves completely in a group in order to proclaim and demonstrate the Kingdom of God.

To be clear, all Christians are outsiders. Having been sent by the most High God, we go as "ambassadors"[12] of Christ, citizens of the "household of God"[13] to live among people who are "alienated and hostile" to Him.[14] Even the Christian who ministers among the same social group for years can never have complete fellowship with

---

12 2 Corinthians 5:20.

13 Ephesians 2:19.

14 Colossians 1:21.

unbelievers.[15] For this reason, the missionary always considers himself to be observing, joining, and influencing from the outside.

Our model, of course, is Christ himself, who "emptied himself, by taking the form of a servant, being born in the likeness of men, being found in the likeness of men. And being found in human form, he humbled himself by becoming obedient to the point of death."[16] The Incarnation of the Son is the highest example of mission — the deliberate crossing of cultural boundaries in order to translate the gospel into the context of others. Incarnation means putting oneself in the shoes of another in order that the gospel might be communicated.[17]

As previously discussed in the chapter on "Identifying Persons of Peace," Jesus sent 72 of His followers on a short-term mission trip instructing them to find their place on His mission by "speaking peace." The idea was that if the missionary is welcomed in, that's where he should stay and concentrate his efforts. This is a good guide for joining a tribe, and exactly the strategy Paul seemed to have employed as he "became all things to all people" so that some may be saved.[18]

Joining a tribe can be very difficult and take a long time. It requires you to be a student of culture and to deliberately expose yourself to those things that influence the tribe. In order to embed yourself in an *oikos*, you must leave your preferences and comforts, and, to a certain extent, leave behind much of your cultural identity. It means deliberately changing your lifestyle in order to identify with others. To join a tribe, you must read the books, watch the films, and wear the clothes that shape the tribe.

Usually, despite your best efforts to join a tribe, you will never truly be considered a full member of a tribe. At best, you can hope to be considered an "acceptable outsider."[19] The reason for this is simple: as new creatures, we are set apart by Christ in us.[20] Add to this the fact that almost everyone already has some social network — group(s) of

---

15 2 Corinthians 6:14.

16 Philippians 2:5–8.

17 For a better explanation of incarnational living, see Frost, *Exiles*, 54–56.

18 1 Corinthians 9:19–22.

19 This term was used by Donald Larson in his 1984 book, *Guidelines for Barefoot Language Learning*. Here, we apply the term to even those Christians operating in same- and near-cultures.

20 "I in them and you in me, that they may become perfectly one, so that the world may know that you sent me and loved them even as you loved me" (John 17:23).

friends they have known since grade school who have a profound influence on their lives. Most people aren't out looking for friends, especially among people who are clearly from outside their tribes. Knowing that you will, to a certain degree, always be an outsider should shape your approach to mission.

Because people are tribal, missionaries tend to focus on "group-building" approaches to ministry. Many missionaries want to form new groups around themselves. "If, despite all the effort, we still can't join a tribe," the missionary seems to think, "we might as well start new ones." So many missionary efforts begin with the socially unattached.[21] When a person transplants to another place, the first thing he does is try to find/build a tribe. It is human nature to be part of community; however, our experience is that not everyone has an *oikos*. Foreigners, outsiders, and new arrivals to a city can be quite disconnected as a result of being without an *oikos*.

Jesus Himself created something of an *oikos* in recruiting a ragtag band of fishermen, tax collectors, and separatists. Forming groups isn't always a bad thing, but creating new tribes can have its downsides. Creating new tribes can be destructive of the existing social network and threaten to extract people from their existing circles. Missionary strategy must recognize that people are likely already grouped. They've been friends since elementary school, neighbors, business partners, extended families, and people with common interests. These connections are far too valuable to lose simply to make the missionary's job easier.

Another option is to indirectly lead a tribe through "shadow-pastoring." This means positioning yourself to constantly influence by teaching individual tribe members this is what the Bible says, and then encouraging them to ask one another, "How does that look in our tribal context?" The idea is that the missionary never holds any sort of authority over the group and may never even meet with the group as a whole. Instead, he deliberately remains in the background, teaching, challenging, warning, and encouraging the group toward Christ.

## When *Oikos* Church Happens

---

21 The socially unattached are not the same as the marginalized, such as outcasts, widows, and orphans. It is the church's job to care for "the least of these." This isn't just kind and merciful, it's good missiology. Many of those who are overlooked and oppressed are socially well-connected. Their public conversion to Christ can have far-reaching influence into a community.

We had been in Spain just over a year when we started studying the Bible with a small group of Spanish friends (believers and non-believers) who had invited us into their tribe. About six months later, we were meeting as a house church. I remember our first meeting as though it were yesterday. My wife and I were nervous although we had entertained these friends in our home dozens of times.

Having grown up in church, I knew how boring and irrelevant church could be. Concerned about reminding them of the negative experiences many Spaniards have in the Catholic Church, we were determined to keep things simple. I planned a short, gospel presentation and a prayer. My wife, who was only just learning to play the guitar, prepared to lead the group in a worship song or two.

Our friends arrived and for the first thirty minutes or so, everything was normal. We talked about politics, religion, current events, and sports. Then, it was time to begin our worship service. I cleared my throat and opened my Bible. The conversation stopped, the room became uncomfortably quiet.

I rushed through the sermon I'd carefully prepared and translated into Spanish. Looking back, I'm pretty sure I said, "Christ died for our fish" instead of "Christ died for our sin." Our friends respectfully listened, but we could tell that things had changed. An awkward silence resulted in an air of formality like when a friend tries to sell Amway at a party.

Then my wife and I sang. Of course, we had intended for the entire group to sing together — we'd even printed out the lyrics for everyone. But this was clearly a show we were putting on for our friends. We didn't so much sing with them as at them. My wife played clumsily (but beautifully!). I did my best to channel my inner baritone. It's hard to hide your tone-deafness when you are six people in the living room of a tiny Spanish apartment. It was excruciating.

When the last chorus had been sung, I quickly prayed. Everyone instinctively echoed my "amen," and proceeded to clap for us. They applauded like parents at an elementary school play.

Despite our best efforts to keep things simple, we'd ruined the environment of casual, yet meaningful discussion we'd always enjoyed with our friends. As informal as our "service" had been, it was still far too formal for it to make sense to the tribe. We had foisted a foreign expression of worship upon our friends, and they didn't know what to do with it.

We were faced with a decision: either continue to perform this sort of church service for the group until they learned to worship through it, or walk them through the passages of Scripture that speak about the *ekklesia* and let them decide how that translated into the culture of their tribe. It was about that time when we stumbled upon 1 Corinthians 14:26: "What then, brothers? When you come together, each one has a hymn, a lesson, a revelation, a tongue, or an interpretation. Let all things be done for building up."

This verse was very good news to our fledgling church. It meant that we could continue doing what the tribe had been doing for years — gathering regularly to encourage one another and process new information — but now with Christ as our motivation. The next time we got together for worship, everyone came prepared with something to edify the church. Some brought a verse or passage of Scripture while others brought a topic of discussion or a question for us to ponder. One made a list of things our group could pray about. A couple of the men came ready to teach, the women had picked out some songs to sing. Everyone brought something, and the result was a well-balanced time of worship in which we all participated according to our gifting.

# HOW TO IDENTIFY TRIBES

The identification of tribes among a people or city requires both observation and personal interaction. In order to organize those observations, it is helpful to use Myers' four spaces of belonging—public, social, personal, and intimate—as an organizing framework.[22] The less personal levels of belonging, the public and the social, are more easily identified through observation. The personal and intimate levels, however, can only be identified through interviews and conversation.

### 1. Public space tribes tend to be expressed openly

Membership to these tribes usually has a low barrier to entry, and provides only a superficial, yet important, level of social connectivity. Harley-Davidson owners may have similar experiences, but riding the same make of motorcycle doesn't mean they actually know one another. Nevertheless, enthusiasts tend to identify themselves primarily in terms

---

22 We recognize that here we are using Myers' framework beyond his purposes in *The Search to Belong*. Our interest here is the identification of a person's tribal affinities.

of being Harley riders. Look for how people identify themselves as fans, supporters, or members:

- sports teams (New York Giants, Atlanta Braves, Manchester United Soccer Club)
- product users (Apple Mac Computer users, Jeep Wrangler owners, Ralph Lauren wearers)
- political parties/cause activists (Free Tibet, The Republican National Convention, Sierra Club, PETA)

Most of these affinities can be detected through observation. Further insight may be gained by asking open-ended, probing questions, "Why does this person desire to express his connection to this tribe publicly?"

## 2. Social space connections tend to have more specific meaning for a person's tribal identity

Members connect out of a sense of who they want to be and how they want their peers to regard them. Watch for how individuals identify with and through:

- city/neighborhood of residence (housing addition, district, or location)
- subcultural affinity (style of dress, consumer habits, media influence)
- career path/universities attended (job titles, fields, areas of study)
- social clubs/activities (fraternities, committees, associations)

These tribal connections require some level of interpretation. For example, an individual may pay particular attention to the way she dresses in order to hide rather than reveal her membership to certain tribes. Listen for references to this level of connections mentioned in conversation.

## 3. The relationship in the personal space is the modern-day equivalent to the social tribe

Here people process new information, develop their worldview, and seek to be community for one another. More often than not, these groups are the primary level of social interaction over the course of the week.

- A small group of close friends (8–16 people)
- Peers at work
- Extended family
- Regular contacts through Facebook, Twitter

How do peers within the tribe respond to these individuals? Do they lead or follow? Do they influence, bringing in ideas from outside the tribe, or do they tend to defend and maintain the tribe's status quo?

## 4. The intimate space is filled by only one or two people and can be very difficult to identify

These "oikoses" are "households" in a stricter sense:

- spouses
- partners
- best friends

This level of belonging may have the greatest impact on a person's major life decisions. Watch for who a person goes to when faced with life-changing events and experiences. Note that the depreciation of marriage as an institution and the common practice of serial short-term romantic commitments make it more and more likely that an individual's spouse/partner does not, in fact, fill this space for an individual.

# HOW TO JOIN A TRIBE

## 1. Study the influences

Expose yourself to whatever influences the tribe. This sort of intentional, deliberate, prayerful exposure is research through immersion. Read the books, watch the films, and rely on local sources of news and information. The goal is to begin to understand why the tribe thinks like it does.

Don't go alone, and have your guard up. It would be foolish to assume that you are somehow impervious to the effects of the influences you're studying. Those things that influence the tribe are full of lies and half-truths. Beware of the harmful, and oftentimes subliminal, effects of things like music, film, and story. Nevertheless, go boldly into the tribes, as you are sent by the Most High God!

## 2. Adopt the rhythm

In order to live out the gospel in word and deed among a particular group of people, you must do all you can to live as they live. You do this by adopting their life "rhythms." Rhythms are the routines, the ebb and flow of life through the calendar year. This includes:

- Diet and mealtimes
- Sleeping schedule
- Work hours, rest hours
- Vacation
- Holidays, festivals, celebrations
- Pace of living, busyness
- Social postures, signs of respect
- Economic identification

Note that there is a clear distinction between rhythm and lifestyle. The lifestyle of non-believers is, by definition, not Christ-centered or God-honoring. To live for whatever they live for or to worship whatever they worship would be to compromise your faith. Instead, reject all ungodliness while intentionally adopting the customs of the tribe in order that tribe members might see in you an example of how their lives might look in Christ.

## 3. Learn the Narrative

By immersing yourself in the culture and rhythm of a tribe you can begin to piece together the patchwork of the tribe's narrative. Influential themes will be woven together with rites and rituals to form the overarching story that shapes the outlook of the tribe. Here, you'll find bridges and barriers to the communication of the gospel. Within the narrative, you'll see where the tribe might be seeking for reconciliation with the Creator. It is here that you can begin to understand just how the gospel is good news to this tribe.

# CONTEXTUALIZATION

[chapter 8]

BY CALEB CRIDER

Si do ta thërrasin, pra, atë, të cilit nuk i besuan? Dhe si do të besojnë tek ai për të cilin nuk kanë dëgjuar? Dhe si do të dëgjojnë, kur s'ka kush predikon? Dhe si do të predikojnë pa qenë dërguar? Siç është shkruar: "Sa të bukura janë këmbët e atyre që shpallin paqen, që shpallin lajme të mira!"[1]

Unless you're fluent in Albanian, the above text probably means nothing to you. It's likely that your eye simply skipped ahead to this section, written in English, which you clearly can read and understand. Unfortunately, that paragraph written in Albanian happens to be a message intended for you.[2]

Now we have a problem. Have I delivered the message? Yes. I began my chapter with a clear presentation of its contents. Nevertheless, something must be done with this message in order for communication to occur: translation. For you to even begin to understand the message, it must be put into a language you can understand. Only then can you reasonably be expected to comprehend, consider, and respond to the message.

All communication requires some effort, but we do most of this subconsciously. For example, I want to invite my neighbors to a cookout. I have to think about how best to communicate that message. Do I leave a note on their doors? Do I call? Send an email? Text? What about a good, old-fashioned face-to-face conversation? We don't usually put too much time into choosing the medium of our communication because we're operating within our own culture. We know, more or less, how our neighbors think.

Nevertheless, the communication process doesn't end there. No matter how I choose to relay the invitation, I have to word the message for clarity. We know that an invitation should include the basics, like what the event is, where it will take place, and when. Without this information, an invitation is pretty much useless. Most of the time, we don't really have to think too much about this. We understand that the details are what we're trying to share.

If we really wanted to break down the process of inviting people to a cookout, though, we could come up with several steps that we may

---

1 Romakëve 10:14-15. Albanian Bible.

2 The message, written in Albanian, is taken from Romans 10:14–15: "How then will they call on him in whom they have not believed? And how are they to believe in him of whom they have never heard? And how are they to hear without someone preaching? And how are they to preach unless they are sent? As it is written, 'How beautiful are the feet of those who preach the good news!'"

not even be aware of. What does the medium say about the message? Would it be inappropriate to send a marching band to the homes of invitees to herald the advent of our backyard cookout? If I send an email, do I write one message to send to everyone on the guest list, or do I write a personal invitation to each recipient? If I decide to visit my neighbors personally, when do I go (middle of the night?), what do I wear (bathrobe?), and how loudly do I speak (angrily shout?)? When you really think about it, a lot goes into communicating even the simplest of messages. The more important the message, the more deliberate we want to be in our communication of it. Communicating an important message across cultural barriers requires that we give thought to each step in the process.

## Cultural Translation

Contextualization is the translation of the gospel from one culture to another. More than just converting the good news into an appropriate language for our audience, mission requires that we interpret the message of the Kingdom into other cultures through word and deed. Missiologist Charles R. Taber gave this definition: "Contextualization is the effort to understand and take seriously the specific context of each human group and person on its own terms and in all its dimensions — cultural, religious, social, political, economic — and to discern what the gospel says to people in that context."[3] It isn't enough to simply disseminate the information of the gospel; we must also demonstrate what salvation in Christ alone means for those to whom we have been sent.

For the sake of mission, contextualization means adjusting how we communicate the gospel so that people do not need to join a new culture in order to hear and understand the message. This is why Jesus instructed us to "go and make disciples of all nations"[4] instead of saying, "go make first-Century, Greek-speaking, Roman-ruled Jews of all nations." This is also why Paul was careful to "become all things to all people, that by all means"[5] some would be saved. Our mission is not to

---

3 Taber, *Contextualization*, 146.

4 Matthew 28:19–20.

5 1 Corinthians 9:19–23.

export a culture, but to infect[6]  existing cultures with what always proves to be a radically countercultural gospel.

Some may ask why we don't "de-contextualize" the gospel– that is, cleanse it of our cultural biases and distill it to some pure, acultural form. But the gospel cannot be interpreted outside of culture. There is no acultural expression of Christianity. Pursing a gospel without culture would be like developing a language without words, symbols, or signs. Culture provides us the tools, such as language, logic, relationships, and experience that allow us to know God and follow Him in community. This is why Christ entered into culture in order to demonstrate God's love and provision for humanity. We call this incarnation: putting flesh on the message. The Son wasn't the only one who incarnates the good news. As Christ's body, we — the church — are to do the same wherever we are. Missiologist David Bosch insisted "If we take the incarnation seriously, the Word has to become flesh in every new context."[7]

God is glorified by a diversity of human culture. This is a recurring theme throughout Scripture, and we can see God's glory in diversity in Genesis 11 and 12. In Genesis 11, we read that humanity had become unified in their efforts to make a name for themselves by building a tower. God intervened by confusing their language, thereby creating many cultures of one. He scattered them across the face of the earth, leaving them isolated and cut off from their own kind. It is in humanity's weakness that God's power is shown to be perfect.[8]  God demonstrated His greatness and power over humanity by dividing them into distinct cultures.

God did not leave the newly-divided nations without hope. In Genesis 12, we read about God's covenant with Abraham to bless all the peoples of the earth through him. Here, God reveals a little more about His plan; just as He scattered all men across the earth, He would one day gather His people unto Himself and send those people out after the scattered and hopeless nations. His every interaction with humanity is done so that the nations might see His power and provision. God's Revelation to John shows the ultimate ending of the

---

6 In his classic work, *Mere Christianity*, C.S. Lewis referred to Christianity as the "good infection," a radical heart change that spreads from person to person like a virus. Here, I'm using that same imagery to illustrate the inside-out change that the gospel produces when it's spread without a cultural packaging. Lewis, *Mere Christianity,* 176–177.

7 Bosch, *Transforming Mission,* 21.

8 2 Corinthians 12:9.

story: a multitude from every tribe, tongue, and nation gathered around the throne to worship the Most High God.[9] Furthermore, God left these newly-formed people groups with the collective memory of His provision. As we read in Romans 1, humanity once knew Him, but willfully exchanged the glory of the immortal God for idols.[10] Even still people everywhere are left with a sense that something is not right. All people everywhere wrestle with deeper questions of justice, meaning, hope, beauty, and love. The longing for freedom and peace and purpose —to know and be known by the Creator—is further testimony of God's heart for the nations. Contextualization is our part in the redemption of humanity through the cultures He created.

## The Contextualization Debate

While contextualization is indeed basic to missiology, it has been the topic of passionate conversation in the world of missions for generations. Virtually no one argues that we should not contextualize at all, but there is great debate about the extent to which we should adapt to individual customs and cultures. Some missiologists assert that contextualization can easily become a distraction from the bold proclamation of the gospel. Others argue that contextualization should be central to mission, that our job as ambassadors of Christ to the nations is to overcome every cultural barrier to the gospel.

This debate isn't just academic; it has serious implications for the daily work of the missionary in every field. Missionaries who don't make contextualization a priority spend much less time learning local languages or adopting local customs. Missionaries who value contextualization, on the other hand, tend to begin their ministries by doing lots of research and taking time to build relationships with nationals. Godly, passionate, and intelligent men and women around the world have taken very different approaches to contextualization.

I want to be clear: Contextualization is not an attempt to "water down" the gospel for the comfort of the hearers. The goal of contextualization is clarity. We don't want our careless methods of presenting the gospel to obscure the offense or the hope of our message of Christ alone. Our message, a call to repentance and obedience to the Lord Jesus Christ, does not change. How we communicate that

---

9 Revelation 7:9.

10 Romans 1:18–25.

message, however, takes some creativity, understanding, and effort on our part.

Some may misunderstand the call to contextualization as searching for the "right way" to present the gospel. Fortunately, the power of the gospel is not dependent upon our presentation of it. People don't need us; they need Christ! We consistently fumble to find appropriate ways to make disciples, but ultimately, we rest in the knowledge of the fact that Christ goes with us. There is no single "correct way" to present the good news. Our love, patience, and presence will point people to the Creator who speaks their language and sees them where they are.

This is why Jesus responded differently to His various audiences. Sometimes, He spoke in parables that actually veiled His message to some who were listening.[11] He told Nicodemus that he must be "born again" in order to see the Kingdom of God.[12] Jesus told the Rich Young Ruler that he must "Go, sell all that you have and give to the poor" in order to be saved.[13] By contextualizing the gospel, Jesus wasn't making it easier for the man to follow Him, but He was making it easier for the man to understand the cost.

## Over- and Under-Contextualization

The conversation around contextualization is not whether to engage in it or not, but rather to what degree will we contextualize? To illustrate the perspectives around the discussion, Fuller Theological Seminary missions professor Dean Gilliland suggests that different missionary approaches fall along a continuum of contextualization. On one extreme, we have those who under-contextualize; they obscure the message by not doing enough to ensure that the gospel is clearly communicated across cultures. On the other extreme, we find those who go too far in contextualization, essentially making the message sound so familiar to existing culture that people simply apply a veneer of Christianity to their paganism.[14] This is called "syncretism," and we see it expressed in cultures who simply rename their idols with Christian names.

---

11 Matthew 13:36–43.

12 John 3:1–15.

13 Mark 10:17–27.

14 Gilliland, *The Word Among Us*, vii.

Syncretism is a very real problem on mission fields worldwide. When people adopt Christianity without abandoning their idols, the gospel is diluted. Many famous misunderstandings of the message can be traced back to insufficient contextualization. Take, for example, the discovery and conquest of the New World 500 years ago. Explorers were sent out by their kings and by the church, to claim new territories for "God and country."

The explorers landed in the Americas with two common religious images to help them communicate the divine authority under which they sailed.[15] To illustrate the miracle of the Incarnation, they carried a painting of the Nativity — the baby Jesus in a manger with His mother Mary caring for Him. Likewise, they depicted the *Pietá* (the events just after Christ's crucifixion) — Mary mourning over Jesus' lifeless body. The combination of the armed and powerful "missionaries" bearing two images of what seemed to be a powerful woman caring for her needy and helpless son reminded the native Americans of their Mother Earth mythology. They renamed Mother Earth "Mary" and thus the syncretistic Cult of the Virgin was born. The means affects the message, and unless we're intentional and intelligent about contextualization, our message will be obscured by our favorite method of sharing the gospel.

In my own ministry, I've been guilty of both under- and over-contextualization. There have been times when my frustration with cultural differences led me to fall back on a good old-fashioned moralism that sounded a lot more like American folk religion than the universal gospel of Scripture. Other times, I found myself being so concerned with finding the contextually-appropriate way to talk about Jesus that I never actually got around to sharing the good news at all.

Despite the modern missionary's best intentions, over-contextualization is a real problem on the mission field. Often a cross-cultural worker can become so focused on acculturating to local customs that he loses entirely that "otherness" that made his message seem so radically different from what the culture otherwise had to offer. Sometimes the contextualization requires a sort of strategic dissonance.

For example, it isn't by chance or laziness that English translators of the Scriptures have, at times, chosen to *transliterate* rather than *translate* biblical Hebrew and Greek into English. The word "angel" isn't an English word at all, but an anglicized version of the ancient Greek word, *angelos*. A close approximation of the meaning of *angelos* would

---

15 Marzal, *The Indian Face of God in Latin America.*

be "messenger," and many Bible translations chose to use that word.[16] But something about the common word "messenger" fails to communicate the glory of the God-sent messengers we read about in Scripture. Instead, scholars introduced the word "angels" into the English vocabulary and taught people its meaning. Likewise, contextualization might sometimes require the missionary to transliterate into his host culture. It isn't the goal of contextualization to lose the "otherness" of the gospel; it's communicating it faithfully across cultural barriers.

Contextualization is serious business; both extremes of over- and under-contextualization fail to communicate the radical, life-bringing gospel to lost and hopeless people. Ultimately, the work of the missionary is to contextualize enough that recipients of the message can see, hear, and understand it without having to adopt a foreign culture, but not so much that we lose the uniqueness and exclusivity of the gospel of Jesus Christ. It is the missionary's job to overcome cultural barriers to the communication of the gospel. This will necessarily look different according to unique cultural and subcultural contexts. We can begin to wrestle with just how to do this by turning to the Cultural Distance Scale:

CULTURAL DISTANCE SCALE

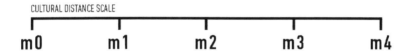

m0     m1     m2     m3     m4

The scale, proposed by missiologist Ralph Winter in 1974,[17] illustrates the challenge of communicating Christ across cultures. The left side of the scale (m0), represents a believer sharing the gospel with someone who completely shares his culture and worldview. This might be a sibling, neighbor, or childhood friend. This is the purest form of evangelism, in that a Christian can share the gospel in much the same way he received it.

Moving along the scale to the right, we see significant cultural barriers (represented by the m's) to the communication of the good

---

16 Logos Apostolic Church of God and Bible College, "Greek Word Study on ἄγγελος."

17 Winter, "The Highest Priority: Cross-Cultural Evangelism."

news. These would be things like language, cultural mores, deeply-held prejudices, idolatry, and the like. Each significant barrier moves us further down the scale, increasing the cultural distance from the missionary to his audience. Naturally, we may think in terms of ethnicities or nationalities, but significant barriers may come in the form of subcultures, socio-economic backgrounds, or family experience. Greater cultural distance requires greater degrees of contextualization.

Lottie Moon, missionary to the Chinese in the late 1800s, was considered radical in her efforts to contextualize.[18] Unlike her peers on the mission field who retained much of their Western culture and lifestyle, Moon adopted the Chinese style of dress and, though it often made her sick to do so, ate traditional Chinese food. These might not seem like groundbreaking efforts, but they were greatly debated among international missionaries of her day. Moon found that simply dressing the part reduced the cultural distance between her and the Chinese by one; eating the food by another. She therefore gladly abandoned her comforts in order that some might be saved.

When we don't contextualize, we end up exporting our culture and methodologies rather than the gospel of the Kingdom. Failure to contextualize is why, on any given Sunday, you can walk into villages in Africa or India and find churches that look just like those of the American South in the1950s. It's why Christianity around the world today has become synonymous with American, capitalist, pop-culture, and materialism. Without contextualization, we spread a gospel of "Christ-plus-our-culture" which, of course, is a false gospel.

### Contextualize for Whom?

Contextualization doesn't begin with the missionary, but with the audience.

A few years a go, a missionary church planter was sent by his church to work among a people group in North Africa. According to the demographic research he'd seen, the people there were 99.9% Muslim. In an effort to begin to contextualize the gospel, the young missionary set out to learn about Islam by reading the Koran and studying Islamic history. He figured this would help him relate to Muslims and find cultural bridges to share the gospel.

---

18 Allen, *The New Lottie Moon Story*, 158–159.

Over time, the missionary began to engage young men in the city to talk about matters of faith. He quoted Mohammad and argued the tenets of Islam. These conversations were never fruitful, and the missionary realized something about his people: they were only nominally Muslim. They didn't know the first thing about Islam, the Koran, or Mohammed. But in order to stick to the contextualization script he'd developed beforehand, the missionary found himself teaching people what they, as Muslims, were supposed to believe. That way, he could begin to argue his case for faith in Christ. Contextualization does not begin with statistics or assumptions; it begins with people.

Had the young missionary spent time in conversation with his North African neighbors, he would have learned that this oppressed minority group needed to hear about freedom in Christ, and about His faithfulness. Had he been listening, he would have heard the people's cry for justice, peace, and identity. These things can be found in Christ. That is good news. Instead, the missionary only taught Islam and rehashed age-old debates. He contextualized for a people that didn't exist at the expense of those who did.

Contextualization requires the missionary to look for the most basic social unit. This would be the largest grouping of people with no significant internal barriers to the communication of the gospel. In some cases, this group might be an ethnolinguistic people group. In other cases, it may be a population segment, clan, village, or urban tribe. People group themselves in any number of ways: geography, economics, affinity, trade, common experience, etc. Contextualization means considering the language, identity, and culture of each of these groups and adjusting our presentation of the gospel in such a way that clearly communicates how the gospel is good news to that group.

Contextualization is more than verbal communication. The missionary must consider how his actions may communicate (or contradict) the message. Denial of self may look quite different from one culture to the next, as may stewardship, blessing, or even personal holiness. Whether it was turning over the tables in the temple, performing signs and wonders, or carrying His cross to Golgotha, it wasn't only Jesus' words that communicated His message, it was His actions. This is why we must proclaim the gospel in word and deed, that others would see our good deeds and glorify God.[19]

---

19 1 Peter 2:11–12.

A college student from Texas was sent by her church as a semester missionary to Spain. Right away, she started meeting young Spanish women who readily accepted her into their social group. The group invited the American student out to dinner, then to a bar, and then to a *discoteca*. Having never actually been in a bar or dance club made her extremely nervous, but she recognized the rare opportunity to spend so much time with Spanish students in their normal environment, and happily went along. Throughout the night, the missionary spoke boldly about her faith. She prayed with the girls, and called them to repentance and life in Christ.

The next day, the college student called home to share the news with her family back in Texas. She told them about the previous night's adventure, and about the rare opportunity she'd been given to share and live the gospel. Rather than rejoicing with her, the young missionary's family was appalled. Her mother was shocked that she had gone into a bar and a night club. "You've ruined your witness!" the mother lamented, disappointed that her daughter could be so easily influenced to compromise her morals. The student apologized to her mother, and never hung out with the Spanish girls again.

What looks like holiness in one culture is not holiness in another. The mother was wrong to rebuke her daughter, who should have been encouraged as an incarnational witness among Spanish students. What the mother didn't realize, and the daughter failed to communicate, is that a "bar" in Spain is not like a "bar" in Texas. A *discoteca* in Madrid isn't the same as a seedy nightclub in Dallas. These were the centers of Spanish social activity. In Spain, no one sees Jesus in you simply because you don't go into bars. In fact, if you don't go into those places, it's likely Spaniards won't really see you at all.

## Christians Are Outsiders

In many ways, missionaries in international contexts have it much easier than ministers and church planters operating in their "home" cultures. When you're clearly the outsider, you act like a guest. You don't assume you have the credibility, authority, or cultural insight that would give you influence. As an outsider, you can't afford to make assumptions about what people believe or whether or not they understand what you're trying to say. You're careful about how you communicate, and if you don't listen carefully, you'll be lost and frustrated.

It turns out that all Christians everywhere are necessarily outsiders — even those who were born and raised in the same communities in which they live today. In Christ, our citizenship is moved from earthly kingdoms to the Kingdom of God. This is why Paul encourages the church at Philippi not to set its mind on earthly things because "our citizenship is in heaven"[20] and why he reminds the Ephesians they were once outcasts, but in Christ they are "citizens in the household of God."[21] Peter implores believers, "as sojourners and exiles," to abstain from sin, which discredits our testimony. As outsiders, then, we follow Christ's example and incarnate the gospel among those to whom we've been sent.

Anyone who has attempted to contextualize the gospel among a people quickly realizes that we can never expect to fully be insiders. A missionary to India may live, dress, and eat like an Indian — he may even become fluent in Hindi — but he will never be Indian. The most we can expect is to be "acceptable outsiders."[22] Nevertheless, a missionary does what he can to minimize the differences between himself and those around him in order to proclaim and incarnate the gospel with clarity.

The goal of contextualization is the communication of the gospel that will result in disciples being made and organized into reproducible, indigenous churches. We do this because our Lord modeled this behavior for us, and then commanded us to do the same. He is glorified in human diversity as His gospel brings life to every tribe, tongue, and nation.

# HOW TO CONTEXTUALIZE

### Learn the culture

As we've mentioned, contextualization begins with culture. As a missionary, armed with a deep knowledge of the unchanging, universal truth of Scripture, you must dive into deliberate study of the host

---

20 Philippians 3:20.

21 Ephesians 2:19.

22 The term "acceptable outsider" is used by sociologists to define the highest social status that may be attained by someone who isn't native to a group. It was made popular by Donald Larson in his book, *Guidelines for Barefoot Language Learning*.

culture. This is best done through immersion. In order to understand a group of people, you must live among them.

A key part of culture is **language**. In cases where you're working among people who speak an entirely different language from yours, you must devote the time and effort into learning the grammar, accent, and use of the local language. But even when you're working among people who seem to speak your language, you've got to be mindful of the way people talk. Is there a difference between how they talk about serious things versus how they talk about the mundane? Do the words you would normally use to communicate the gospel already have other meanings or negative connotations here? You need to study the local language in order to even begin to answer these questions and then to develop creative solutions.

## Make a map

Compile the findings of your research, interviews, and experiences in a format that will facilitate your understanding and ability to share the insight you gain. Note those things that might be relevant to your understanding of how people communicate and interact with one another. Conduct cultural exegesis to find the bridges and barriers to the gospel that already exist within culture.

Note: Culture learning cannot be done from an office chair in front of a computer. It takes more than a Google search to understand people. Only through personal interaction will they become people, not statistics or projects.

## Proclamation in word and deed

Constantly ask, "How is the gospel 'good news' to these people?" (Keeping in mind that, as with the Rich Young Ruler, the "good news" may sound very much like bad news.) Remember that people don't see Jesus in you because you don't smoke, drink, etc. Find out what would help them see Jesus in you.

Practice both presence and proclamation. Incarnation demands both a verbal and behavioral witness. In 1 Thessalonians 2:8, Paul writes that his team was "ready to share not only the gospel of God but also our own selves, because you [the church at Thessalonica] had become very dear to us."

Make it a habit to tell people what the Bible says, then ask, "How would this look in your culture?" This helps to establish the Scriptures, and not the missionary, as the authority for the practice of our faith. It also challenges disciples to learn to express Christianity in their own contexts. Of course, in order to do this you need to know what the Bible says. Commit to studying the Scriptures deeply and often. You also need to be self-aware of your biases and cultural baggage. Do what you can to overcome your own biases, prejudices, and comforts.

Trust that the Holy Spirit is at work and speaks their language. Allow for "mistakes." God's global mission involves you, but it doesn't depend on you. Never assume that your strategy, words, or personality are enough to win people to Christ, because they aren't. Do your best, and pray for salvation to come to the people.

Never stop contextualizing. Culture is dynamic and ever-changing, and so are our missionary strategies. Just when you think you've found a good way to talk about Jesus to a people, they change. Political climates, social movements, and societal trends are constantly in flux. Influences come and go. Your efforts toward contextualization aren't just to a people, but to a people in a specific time and place. Contextualization isn't a task to be finished, but a posture to be assumed. It's our identity. Go boldly to make disciples in culture by teaching them to obey all that Christ commanded us. Be encouraged — He goes with us always, even to the end of the age.

# PURSUING ALTERNATIVE PATHS

[chapter 9]

BY WADE STEPHENS

Jim worked for a large multinational company when he and his wife Shelly felt led to move overseas on mission.[1] Though his company had offices in the city where they were planning to move, Jim chose to join a mission-sending agency and leave his old job. During the process, the 30-something couple met with a missionary who encouraged them to consider a transfer with Jim's employer. A transfer would meet financial needs, provide the essential work permit, and provide access to a large number of nationals. Jim and his wife, however, were committed to being "full-time missionaries" so they could devote all of their time and energy to evangelism, discipleship, and church planting. The couple felt that going through a mission agency would enable them to work out the financial details and work permit, and that having access to nationals and a credible reason for interacting with them would be something they would overcome.

Six months later, the missionary who had provided counsel encountered this couple again overseas. They had studied the language and were looking for ways to connect with nationals. Finding it more difficult than expected to start relationships with people who were outside of the church, Jim expressed some regret for not having pursued the possibility of a job transfer with his previous company. He shared that working for a company would have given him both a credible, understandable reason for being in the country and a natural way to enter into relationship with others.

Over the past couple of years, many people have shared with me their desire to be on mission internationally. The majority of these people were not seminary-educated. Instead they worked in a range of vocations, including engineer, pilot, entrepreneur, salesman, accountant, etc. Often these conversations begin with the would-be missionary sharing his or her desire to go as a full-time missionary through his or her church or a mission agency. Some continue down that path. Some give up, at least for a while. Yet others begin to see and pursue opportunities to use their vocation as a way to be a missionary.

As Jim and Shelly experienced, there are four challenges that missionaries typically encounter today. *Credibility* is an issue in many places. A job title of "missionary" is often a strange and foreign idea to those in another country while the idea of an expatriate working in a company is common. *Accessibility* can be a challenge for a person with the title of missionary, but a person working in the marketplace has

---

1 Names changed to protect identity.

natural and regular interaction with colleagues, suppliers, and customers as well as neighbors and people in the marketplace. The *cost of living* overseas is a prohibitive factor for some, but working as a tentmaker meets or at least helps meet much of the financial needs. Obtaining the *essential documents* such as a visa or work permit is also becoming increasingly difficult for the professional missionary, but marketplace workers usually face less difficulty here.

## Identifying the Paths

Being on mission with God is a journey. It is a marathon that we are to "run with endurance" (Hebrews 12:1). Mission is not a destination, but an ongoing trek for the believer. During this journey, we will take different routes or paths at different points along the way. Both the place we come from and the place to which we are going will have significant bearing on the path that we will take. Though these paths are important, they are not the focus of our travels. The unchanging point of emphasis requires that we continue "looking to Jesus, the founder and perfecter of our faith, who for the joy that was set before him endured the cross, despising the shame, and is seated at the right hand of the throne of God" (12:2). He is the focus. The journey is about our mission with  Him. Alternative paths, strategies, approaches, or tactics are a part of our obedience to Him. Any of these efforts are about His glory, not our own.

There are two broad categories of paths: traditional paths and alternative paths. Both of these categories have multiple expressions. The reason is that Scripture does not prescribe one definitive way to always do mission. Whether a path is traditional or alternative may be identified by examining four features of the mission effort: identity of the missionary, mode of mission, location of mission, and how God provides the resources for mission.

A summary of these four can be broken down as follows:

|  | Traditional Paths | Alternative Paths |
|---|---|---|
| Identity of the missionary | Missionary or full-time minister | Tentmaker or other creative platform |
| Mode of mission | Preaching to others | Interacting with others |
| Location of mission | Worship or evangelistic gathering | Marketplace, homes of non-believers, places where people gather |
| Resources for mission | Funded through the church | Funded through the market |

At the beginning of Acts, we observe Peter using a traditional approach. Unequivocally, this was the leading of the Holy Spirit. On the day of Pentecost, he preached and God-fearing Jews from every nation heard the gospel in their own language and believed. We read that 3,000 were added to their number that day (Acts 2:1-41). Peter was easily identifiable in this story as a preacher, evangelist, or full-time minister. The mode of mission on this occasion was preaching. He employed this method at a spontaneous gathering of devout Jewish men from many nations. This quickly became an evangelistic gathering. The resources for Peter's ministry up to this point had come through the gifts of others as he had followed Jesus. Through use of this traditional approach, Peter was used by God in accomplishing His mission.

Paul used the same approach, especially during his early missionary journeys. But later in his ministry, he stayed in Ephesus for two years investing in some disciples. Because of Paul's efforts to train these believers, "all the residents of Asia heard the word of the Lord, both Jews and Greeks" (Acts 19:10). Just prior to this extended period in Ephesus, Paul lived and worked as a tentmaker, giving him the resources he needed to live, as it were, on mission.

At this point in Paul's ministry, he was making tents, at very least for economic reasons. In addition to providing for his financial needs, his work during the week also provided him opportunity to disciple other believers. Also, based on Paul's normal behavior, he likely shared the hope of Christ with non-believing tentmakers, suppliers, and customers. But Paul did not make tents just as a means of making a living so that he might be able to make some disciples along the way. He was intentional about his choice to work in the marketplace. He shared some powerful concluding thoughts with the Ephesian elders at the end of his two years with them:

> I coveted no one's silver or gold apparel. You yourselves know that these hands ministered to my necessities and to those who were with me. In all things I have shown you that by working hard in this way we must help the weak and remember the words of the Lord Jesus, how he himself said, 'It is more blessed to give than to receive.' (Acts 20:33-35)

In these parting words to his missionary disciples, Paul placed special emphasis on his tent-making work. It was important to him not to be a burden to the church. He also worked to generate funds which allowed him to be a blessing to those in need. Through making tents and giving of his own money, he gave a clear witness of the Messiah who gave Himself away for others. Paul's approach to mission actually amplified, or made more visible, the message of the gospel.

During this period, Paul's mode of mission included training other missionaries as well as interacting with other tentmakers like Aquila and Priscilla, and with people in the city (Acts 18:1-4). He moved his meeting location from the temple to the hall of Tyrannus (Acts 19:8-10). His tent-making would have continued to keep him among other tentmakers and in the marketplace as well. God provided Paul with the financial resources he needed to be on mission through his marketplace work.

It is clear that God used Peter's methodology in Acts 2 and Paul's in Acts 18-19. There is not a right or a wrong approach or path to mission here. The methods can even be mixed, as evidenced by Peter ministering in a home (Acts 10) and Paul preaching or teaching in the temple. All four features of a mission effort do not have to fit exclusively in the traditional or alternative path column. Instead, the Church needs to realize that an informed, effective, and culturally appropriate sending of her people will include both traditional and alternative paths to mission. A sending church needs to utilize different paths in different contexts, both economic and social, based on the giftedness of the one(s) being sent.

### Examining Alternative Paths

Too many Christians view mission as something that can be accomplished only through a traditional approach. If someone wants to go and be on mission, common practice requires that he quit his job, go through extensive training, develop funding avenues, and finally, make the move. But in so many places and niches in the world today, there are professionals, experts, students, and others needed to shine the light of Christ. These "missionaries" need to be recognized, honored, trained, and prayed for as what they are: missionaries. Also, in many parts of the world, full-time missionaries are struggling to find relevance and ways to connect to a lost world. Alternative paths are ways that these various types of missionaries are finding to be on mission in various locations in credible ways. The number of people being sent out through the church using alternative paths is small but growing. Sending churches are beginning to consider alternative paths as the number of people seeking to go on mission increases. Often, we have seen families go on mission in this way without their church being aware. The church needs to send these people. How she equips and sends them out needs to increasingly become a part of their tradecraft.

There is a seemingly endless number of alternative ways to function as a missionary. Categorizing the possibilities helps spur creativity about possible alternative mission strategies.[2] Three types of alternative paths are: secular, creative, and platform strategies. These are not necessarily mutually exclusive, but most approaches tend to fall primarily into one of these three categories.

Secular paths to mission exist where someone gets a *regular* job or studies like a *normal* student and uses her new assignment for mission. Common approaches here include taking a job with an existing company, a non-profit organization, or studying as a university or graduate student for academic credit. Another way to pursue a path in this category is as a business traveler or tourist with purpose. An *intentional traveler* cultivates relationships with the intention of planting the gospel through his travels. This is done by consistently staying in the same hotel and eating in the same cafes over a period of time. Because secular paths are not dependent on donor support, they

---

2 The most widely recognized categorical system of this kind was put forward by Patrick Lai in his book *Tent-making*. It has been an invaluable part of the business as mission conversation. However, to simplify and seek to value approaches a bit differently, I have proposed this new categorization. Lai, *Tent-making*, 21-28.

provide one of the easiest ways to start on mission in terms of funding. This strategy presents a unique opportunity to use existing infrastructure or opportunities to go and make disciples while fulfilling work requirements.

Currently, there are people all over the world utilizing secular paths for mission. This includes embassy personnel, humanitarian relief organizations, university students, engineers, accountants, etc. One example of the secular path is a research scientist who moved with his wife to work with a pharmaceutical company in Switzerland a few years ago. Initially, he was excited about opening a Swiss bank account and working in such a beautiful place in the heart of Europe. After a couple of weeks on the new job, his excitement faded because of the need he saw among his coworkers. He began to have conversations with leaders in Skybridge Community, a group of like-minded people pursuing alternative paths to mission, and in his local church about what it would look like for him to be a missionary.[3] Now he does pharmaceutical research while taking the gospel to those in his spheres of influence and helping with a church plant in his city.

*Creative paths* to mission are those that exist by starting something new. Options here are unlimited. These may be created to meet the needs of an entity (business-driven), people, or place (mission-driven). Creative paths may take the form of a for-profit or non-profit entity. This category offers an opportunity for a business that is already profitable in a line of products or services to open a branch or division in another place. A business can strategically "outsource" a business function to another place. Options here could include traditional outsourcing with intentionality or maintaining control in-house though moving the office to another place in the world. This occurs when a company locates an aspect of its business like information technology or accounting to another part of the globe. Another creative strategy would include starting a new business or non-profit organization that develops around a people or place. Creative paths provide one of the greatest opportunities to dream big strategically in order to develop an avenue that significantly advances the gospel.

One business in Missouri has used creative strategies to start different creative paths for clear mission purposes. One of their initiatives started due to mission-driven needs and the other because of business-driven demands. The first venture arose through employee

---

3 www.skybridgecommunity.net.

connections to an impoverished country in southern Europe. Seeing the need in one of the smaller cities for the gospel to go forward, company leaders helped establish an English-language school. Through the repeated, sustained contact students and adults have with Christ-followers through English-language activities, many have trusted Christ. The company and the language school continue to work with the local church and the students in seeking to disciple these young believers. A second venture for the company began when looking for ways to increase manufacturing capacity. Relocating a key line of product manufacturing to East Asia, the company moved a full-time employee over to work with the manufacturer and to oversee quality control. This employee is in a close working relationship with many in the production process and has seen a number of factory workers begin to follow Christ. U.S. company management continues to make trips to the factory for some business-related reasons, but primarily to take the gospel to the factory owner. Their current business strategy includes continuing to produce quality products and seeing a church planted in the factory with the owner's blessing.

*Platform paths* to mission are jobs, roles, or functions that allow professional missionaries to relate to people in culturally appropriate ways. These paths are for missionaries who are already funded through support, a mission agency, or through personal resources. Using a skill, hobby, or profession, a missionary finds a way to interact with the people he is working among. Platform efforts are usually low in capital requirements which makes them relatively easy to begin and terminate.

Some platform endeavors include agricultural consulting in places around the world including South America and sub-Saharan Africa. Hydroponics is being implemented in parts of Asia. Photography and other arts are being used in various ways in places in Europe. Quality control inspections provide an opportunity for some missionaries in South Asia. Journalism provides an outlet for some in North Africa, the Middle East, and Central Asia.

## Critical Components

One of the challenges with discussions about alternative paths to mission is the vast scope. To date, these conversations have often been referred to as business-as-mission (BAM), *tent-making*, developing a *platform*, and creative access. While the BAM and tent-making designations have referred more to a business approach that does mission, platforms and creative access have been the domain of missionaries developing a business entity or approach to help their mission efforts. However, all of these terms can connote different things to different people. Here we are using the phrase "alternative paths to mission" as this area includes individuals and organizations that have a starting point in mission or business. There is not a right and a wrong path here, as I have seen various efforts advance the gospel. While all of the above can prove helpful, there is one variant that has proved consistently problematic: Halfhearted, undeveloped attempts at pursuing alternative paths to mission do not go well.

After the World Trade Center towers were attacked on September 11, 2001, the ramifications were felt around the world. Many of the universities in other countries to which missionaries previously had had free access to began to close their campuses to them. Non-students and organizations had to apply for permission to be on these campuses. Some missionaries who had been working with universities simply had business cards printed up to gain access. In some places this worked for a season; in other locations it did not. Over time, some universities became more stringent in checking the reason for certain individuals being on a campus. I have seen multiple mission organizations lose access to university campuses for going in under one identity and purpose but then doing something else. Since the missionary viewed himself only as a missionary, he did not fulfill the role he had promised. Many have referred to this as a bait-and-switch tactic. This has led to a loss of access to some universities and organizations. Additionally, partial attempts have caused some missionaries to be expelled from a country and have their visas revoked.

A friend of mine tells the story of a bait-and-switch like this:

> Two days after arriving in Western Europe, our team leader took my wife and me to the immigration office to register for our residence permits. On our way to the government building, the veteran missionary warned us to be careful what we said in the waiting room. "The office will be full of all sorts of people," I remember him saying, "and some of them really don't like Americans."
>
> We had been prepared for anti-Americanism. It was no secret that the U.S. wasn't necessarily loved by everyone else in the world. Our missionary training had covered security — what to say and

do in the eventuality of antagonism or worse. Still, we were happy to have an experienced worker with us, just in case.

The trip to the immigration office was an adventure in waiting. Wait until the officials finish their cigarettes and decide to open for the day. Wait for the proper forms. Wait until you're given a number, and then wait until your number was called. The only thing to do while waiting was to watch the other people in the waiting room. These people, from all around the world, were, in turn, watching us while they waited.

Our team leader took the opportunity to continue our orientation to local culture. As he told us about his interactions, both positive and negative, with the people of the city, we noticed a young woman on the other side of the lobby watching and listening intently to our conversation. After some time, the woman came over to us with a huge smile on her face. "I couldn't help but overhear your conversation," she said, "I'm just so happy to find fellow Americans here!"

I quickly replayed our conversation with our team leader in my mind. Had we been negative about the people? Had we complained? Had we compromised the security of our colleagues by talking openly about sensitive information? My wife and I ignored the woman and turned to our team leader. He would know how to handle this eavesdropper.

"What do you do here in country?" the woman asked. For the new missionary, it was difficult to know how to answer this question. The answer was complicated; we had been trained to give out only necessary information regarding our presence in country. While it was technically legal for us to be missionaries there, the social climate made it necessary for us to have a platform — some secular work that would legitimize our presence there. The problem was that we hadn't yet decided what our platform was to be. Again, we turned to our team leader.

"Me? Well, I'm... we, um... er..."

Clearly experience on the field didn't make the question any easier to answer.

"I work a lot with schools." he stammered.

The American woman was polite. "Wow, that's terrific! My mother was a teacher when I was a kid. Are you a teacher? Administration?"

"Yeah, I'm sort of like a teacher, but I don't teach. I said I work with schools, not in them!" The TL seemed defensive. We were confused by both his answer and his reaction. Clearly, so was the woman, so he attempted to clarify.

"I'm actually more like a counselor. I help people with their problems."

"A counselor? Like a psychologist? I actually know a marriage counselor here. He's an old family friend. He has a practice in the city center. Maybe you know him?"

"I'm not that kind of counselor." The missionary said awkwardly. "I guess you could say I'm a photographer. I take lots of pictures."

Now things were getting weird. This man had changed careers three times in five minutes. Either he was schizophrenic or a terrible spy. How can a grown man not know why he had moved to Western Europe? My wife and I felt embarrassed, but didn't know how to help. We stared at our shoes and prayed that our number would be called soon.

"A photographer, huh?" the woman said, incredulously.

"Well I do have a really nice camera, but I'm not a professional, by any means."

She actually took a step back away from us, clearly uncomfortable with this strange behavior. She began to look around nervously. I assume she was looking for a police officer or hidden camera crew.

"Actually," the missionary said, now leaning in close and lowering his voice to a whisper, "we're undercover missionaries. This couple just joined our team and I'm leading their orientation."

"Missionaries?" the woman said, unsure of whether to believe him this time, and slightly disappointed that it might have been true. "Interesting," she said, looking us over without looking the least bit interested. She returned to the other side of the room and avoided eye contact with us.

We finished our business at the government building and headed to the university to enroll in language school. As we walked, our team leader said, "Can you believe that girl? What was with the interrogation? Usually, people don't ask so many questions."

Clearly.

When we got home that night, my wife and I talked at length about that experience. Had our team leader received the same training we had? How should we have answered the questions? An encounter like that could have been disastrous for our relationships with locals and could even jeopardize our permission to live there! We were thankful that at least the interaction had been with an American and not with a national. That would have been really bad.

We started language school Monday morning. There were about a dozen students in the class: a couple of Japanese college kids, a Dutch businessman, an elderly German couple, and a few Americans, including the same woman from the immigration office.

For all types of wholehearted attempts to being on mission through creative access, there are five key components to consider.[4] The starting point to doing any type of mission well is to have a *sending church*. The sending church does just that. It sends people out. The sending church commits to pray for them, remember them, visit them when they are discouraged, and help them in whatever ways are needed. Like Paul and Barnabas' relationship with the church in Antioch, these learn from each other and hold each other accountable.[5] When you begin to sense the Holy Spirit calling you to go out, begin conversations with leaders in your church. Like the church in Antioch, this should be the church leaders sending out other leaders in the church to be on mission. Whether you are considering going through a mission organization or directly through your church, this is still a key step. While the commitment may be from the church, it is usually necessary to have small groups that fulfill this commitment. These are the ones who stay in contact with the missionary and share with the larger body praises and needs.

Some sending churches are beginning to lead out in mission. One example is LifePoint Church in Smyrna, TN. They have sent teams with multiple families to two different continents to take the gospel of Jesus Christ. One team is in an urban center in Asia and the other in

---

4 These five key components come from the Skybridge Community. While these are driving factors of Skybridge, these components are not the exclusive domain of Skybridge. Skybridge Community, "About Skybridge."

5 Acts 13:1-3; 14:24-28.

Europe. What is unique about these efforts is that they are not short-term teams. The expectation for these teams is a three-year commitment. Already, some of the families on those teams are looking at longer investments to see the gospel take root in the cities among whom they are living and working.

Second, it is important to have a *job*. For the individual, this is pretty straightforward. Not always easy, but clear enough. Creativity and networking in the job search process are vital for most. A good starting place for creativity is the annually revised book, *What Color is Your Parachute*.⁶ Once again, the many business persons who travel extensively can be in mission through being an intentional traveler. If your job already puts you in the same parts of the world on a regular basis, then having intentionality to stay in the same hotel, eat in the same restaurants, etc., can provide opportunities for you to advance the mission among that people. For an existing business, the job- creation process may mean setting up another location for a certain function like IT, manufacturing, sales, etc. For a missionary or mission agency seeking to enter into a place, then it may require setting up an entity or credible service that is either a for- or non-profit. Involve some entrepreneurial minds in this process. Still another possibility for a full-time missionary in the alternative path job domain may be to function as a *connectionist* who networks with like-minded people. The connectionist interacts with other missionaries in order to know what is happening in the city and with alternative path missionaries to facilitate opportunities to work together.

Third, *training* is essential. Those who have not been intentional in mission before are usually anxious to receive input. For any who may have experience in a traditional approach to mission, coaching from others can provide a healthy alternate perspective to identify ways to live missionally among coworkers. I have had a number of expatriates working at multinational firms in various urban contexts share that they would like to serve as a missionary while living in their new country, but they simply don't know how. These would-be missionaries need mentoring so that they can move forward with confidence and learn from the experience of others. They should be equipped as missionaries who make disciples that make disciples. Through this, the body of Christ can rise up on mission.

---

6 Bolles, "What Color is Your Parachute?"

Fourth, having a local *ministry connection* is desirable. Where possible, seek to come alongside others who are making disciples, starting groups, and planting churches. This may be a local church. In many locations there will be a missionary or national church planter seeking to advance the gospel. If working together is viable, it can encourage all involved.

Fifth, participating in a *community* of like-minded people can be critical. There will be times of frustration and discouragement. Even the most laser-focused committed person can lose sight of the objective in the process. The Great Commission is not a Lone Ranger journey. It is done best in community with encouragement as you share together what God is doing, what you are learning, and lifting each other up in prayer.

## Celebrate

Chuck and Katy were both serving as short-term missionaries in Europe with a mission agency.[7] Their church in the States celebrated these two young people living on mission. Through prayer, sending care packages, and putting their pictures up on the missionary bulletin board, the church supported them. After Chuck and Katy finished their time in Europe and Chuck obtained his MD, they moved to a low-income area in a North African country to be on mission. He was planning to practice medicine while she would write as a freelance author. Together, their income might just be enough to pay the bills. Though the couple viewed themselves as being on mission, their church took their pictures from the bulletin board. Chuck and Katy were no longer viewed as missionaries by those who had rejoiced during their previous overseas departure.

When I first learned of this story, I shook my head in disbelief. Yet since that time I have encountered other churches that have held similar positions. One such church had a family go out from them and plant their lives in an impoverished European country because they had been captivated by the people there who desperately needed God. The church prayed for the family, but was uncertain whether or not to partner with them in any significant way, or to view them as official missionaries sent out from their church. When I met with the mission leaders, I asked if this family had some moral, leadership, or theological

---

7 Names changed to protect identity.

173

issues that would keep them from being qualified as missionaries. The mission team shared that the family was sound morally, had been strong leaders in the church, and that they were very sound theologically. Church leaders were concerned because this family was not affiliated with a particular approved mission-sending agency. Though the church wanted to hold this family up as missionaries, they held back for some time. To this and other churches I would say, "Permission granted!" Partner with those healthy families whom God is compelling to go out on mission. Celebrate what God is doing in their lives and among the people where they plant their lives. But beware because people will be compelled to follow their example. As the church celebrates while sending her best out, more are likely to pursue mission in their workplace and to the nations.

If alternative paths to mission are going to be a key part of mission, then some celebratory changes are essential. First, the church needs to be fulfilling the Great Commission. We are sent as Jesus was sent (John 20:21). In turn, the body of Christ is both the sent and sending church. Like the church in Antioch, we are to be sending out those who will take the gospel to others. Like Paul who often lived as a tentmaker, many today are ready to do the same. The church should encourage those who are ready to give their lives in this way. She should be sending these out with her blessing, training, support, and massive amounts of prayer. She should journey along with those she sends out to encourage and be encouraged by them. To teach and be taught by them. In every way and path possible, the church should view herself as the body of Christ on mission, as the sending church.

Second, mission organizations need to find ways to partner closer with churches and work with those she sends out on mission. Sharing information, resources, expertise, and celebrating what God does through others are key for mission moving forward today. Alternative paths must be given serious consideration for those heading out on mission whether they are sent through a church or a mission agency. Profitable businesses and successful non-profit organizations have on numerous occasions given visa opportunities to full-time missionaries. This is a basic level of partnership for mission agencies, but more is required. Mission organizations need to view those who are starting and running those businesses and non-profits as missionaries also. The agency may be able to train them in mission practices while learning from these other organizations and individuals about running a business or non-profit. Increasing in these types of skills just may help advance mission in the future. While writing this chapter, I learned of a family seeking to go out on mission through a mission agency who were denied visas to a financially challenged European country. The rejection seems to be a result of appearing more missionary-like in intent rather than bringing something of value to the country. Partnership and celebration of alternative paths will be critical to missions moving forward.

Third, seminaries need to advance the idea and practice of alternative paths to mission. Most full-time missionaries have some seminary education. That is a good thing. Theological training is important. But many seminary graduates I have spoken with admit that not all of their education is critical to their daily activities in ministry. Seminaries should identify key aspects for equipping those who are living as marketplace missionaries. Making these basic elements available through an abbreviated semester or some type of distance learning would be a valuable resource to help marketplace workers think more like a missionary.

Additionally, seminaries can educate future pastors on ways to release their marketplace workers on mission. Equipping pastors to equip the mission force that is the church will release countless missionaries at home and abroad. Also, it will elevate the role of those who are missionaries serving through alternative paths. Instead of encouraging those who are called to mission to leave the workplace and pursue full-time missionary status, pastors should be trained to encourage people to investigate and celebrate all possible paths toward mission.

## ALTERNATIVE PATHS: HOW-TO

We have to think analytically to evaluate alternative paths to mission. Alternative paths should be helpful in dealing with the issues of: credibility, accessibility, cost of living and essential documents. When deciding whether or not to pursue an alternative path to mission, the missionary should answer three key determination questions.

• Is there an access issue that needs to be overcome? This can range from getting a visa into a country to whether or not the missionary is able to gain access to a specific people. For example, a missionary sent to work with university students in a place where access to the university is restricted could pose a problem. Through an alternate approach, access issues can disappear. Non-religious visas often provide greater access around the world.

• Is developing relationships with people a challenge? Regardless of the reason, if a missionary is unable to develop meaningful relationships with the lost of a culture, making disciples will be an impossible endeavor. Alternate paths that will cause sustained, significant interaction with a people will be helpful.

• Are the people largely non-responsive to the gospel? Sustained interaction with a people can often foster a pre-discipleship process that will lead to people becoming Christ followers.

If the answer to any of the determination questions is yes, then alternative paths to mission deserve prayer and investigation. Moving forward with a different strategy may make sense, but it must also fit with the Spirit's leading. Pray continually and at this point in the journey, devote extra time to prayer. The next step is to evaluate possible strategies. Evaluating these questions as a team will produce better results. The team will benefit by having at least one strategic thinker and cultural expert. A list of evaluation questions the team should address include:

• Does the strategy fit the people and culture? Would the strategy be considered by nationals as something that would meet their need or benefit them in some way? For example, starting a coffee shop in a developing economy may be of value. Putting a U.S. coffee shop in an Italian urban center, however, would not be too appealing for Italians who take pride in their ability to craft a great cup of coffee.

• Does the strategy enable the missionary to both maintain integrity and operate with wisdom? The strategy being considered should position the missionary as one that can transparently be a Christ-following disciple-maker while positioning the missionary to have influence in society. The influence may come from a position of authority or a humble position of service.

176

• Does the strategy allow for close, sustained interaction with non-believing nationals? Some alternate paths just provide access. This in itself is important and may be sufficient reason for pursuing an alternative path. However, when a strategy provides access and interaction with people on a regular basis, then pre-discipleship opportunities may develop where the lost can begin to observe and consider the gospel. If a strategy develops situations where Christ-centered conversations naturally develop, then this would be an optimal approach.

• Does the strategy positively impact the goal of missions? This question is very similar to the previous, but it is still important. If the path you are considering does not provide interaction with non-believing nationals, then you need to determine how much time will this responsibility take. If you invest 40 hours a week in a job that does not help you initiate relationships with those that are lost, then how much time will you be able to devote to mission? What if the job takes 50 or 60 hours of your time every week? It is my experience that most jobs provide some amount of interaction. However, there are functions like data-entry that may limit time with others. Also, there is an increase in the number of policies companies maintain that prohibit proselytizing and church planting. Usually there are ways to fulfill the policy and be on mission. However, this is something that needs to be prayed through by the sending church and the missionary.

Before committing to move forward, consider these *before-you-jump* questions:

• Is my sending church in agreement about an alternative path? This may require a process of vision casting, but a sending church and, if present, the mission agency should be supportive of an effort or the missionary must reconsider the strategy.

• Does the missionary, mission team, or church possess the necessary expertise and resources to make a particular path viable? Without some level of competence, alternative missions end badly. As the ones bearing the name of Christ, we should seek to excel in all areas so that His glory will be advanced. Because we do everything for the glory of God, efforts done for the purpose of mission should reflect the glory of God through excelling in areas such as products and services.

• Is the disciple-making process reproducible for a future indigenous movement? Whether or not a particular alternate strategy is reproducible may not be an issue, but it is critical that the process of making disciples not be overly-embedded in a strategy. For example, if the missionary selects a creative path of establishing humanitarian relief, how disciples are taught to make disciples would be important. If the disciple-making process happens only as often as food is distributed, then future indigenous efforts will be impossible without ongoing humanitarian relief.

• Has counsel been sought from others that may be more knowledgeable than I am on either the strategy or mission aspect of a possible strategy? The church has incredible wisdom that may provide a more balanced, realistic alternative path to mission.

• Is there a simpler way to meet the goals that we have not tried yet? Any possible traditional path to missions or simpler alternative path should be evaluated as a possibility.

The process of starting well on an alternative path may seem a bit overwhelming. That is probably a good thing to be aware of. However, when working in community with others that are gifted in working through similar processes, the dreaming process can be a lot of fun and may move quicker than you might expect. During the journey, continue to seek the Spirit's leadership. That's essential for any mission endeavor all along the way–from beginning to end.

# PROTECTING INDIGENEITY

[chapter 10]

BY LARRY E. MCCRARY

We arrived at the church early that overcast, fall Sunday morning. An enthusiastic usher handed us bulletins and helped us to our seats on the left-hand side of the sanctuary close to the front near the organ. Not long after we took our seats, the choir, clothed in colorful robes, filed quietly into the loft at the front of the room. The pastor and two deacons followed soon after as the organist played her favorite rendition of Come, Thou Fount of Every Blessing. A quick scan of the room revealed men sharply dressed in suits and ties while women donned their best Sunday dresses. As the prelude concluded, the pastor walked to the pulpit and heartily greeted the congregation with a welcome to the church.

You can probably picture it. You can see faces around the room, hear the melodious tone of the organ, and recognize the voice of the pastor. Most of you reading this book have probably experienced it. A lot. The difference in this story and the one you know is this is not First Church of Most Towns, USA. Rather, this church is located in a large city in Asia. In a city where Mandarin Chinese is the dominant tongue, the pastor teaches in strangely accented English to a congregation struggling to understand him.

This occurrence is not an isolated instance. We hear stories of churches all around the world operating in the very same manner. Imported hymns, architecture, and decorations that mimic American churches, and even English language for public services pervade churches all over the globe. It is not uncommon for the culture of the host country to be completely absent from the worship setting and replaced by mid-century American church culture. Local believers often lack the freedom to explore indigenous (culturally appropriate) expressions of church.

The problem with this type of approach is that churches and missionaries are actually adding a barrier to the gospel by importing culture that has nothing to do with it. By including English language and American church practice in a distinctly non-American setting, the missionary is inadvertently saying that people must become Americans before they can become Christians. Therefore, it is imperative for missionaries to protect indigeneity by properly exegeting the culture and discerning what the church should look like in that context.

## Indigenous

"Indigenous" is an agricultural term that means "generated from within or capable of originating from within the local context."[1] A plant is indigenous if it originates in the place it is found. The opposite of "indigenous" is "exogenous," which is defined as "originating outside of the local environment; foreign, extraneous in origin."[2] A transplanted species is exogenous. A wooded, country road in eastern Tennessee lined with Eastern White Pine or Silver Maple trees is an example of indigenous plant life. Those species are naturally found there. The same road lined with Hawaiian Koa trees or any sort of palm tree, plant life not naturally found in the region, boasts exogenous foliage.

Horticulturist Paola Zannini describes North American native, indigenous plants as any that were growing in North America before the European settlement. She points out that the advantages of native plants are obvious. "Native plants, once established, are more adaptable to our gardens, and they contribute to create an ideal habitat for desirable wildlife such as butterflies and birds."[3] In other words, indigenous gardens thrive easier than those made up of their exogenous counterparts.

Zannini offers a few important steps on growing native plants. Among others, she suggests that garden habitats should reflect the natural environment from which they come. Once such a habitat is created, care should be given for the plants until they are well established and can withstand extreme weather conditions.[4]

These lessons on indigeneity learned from horticulture have an important application in mission, particularly as we plant churches among definitive peoples and within certain cultures. Indigenous churches are fellowships that are native to their local soil where they can grow, thrive, and reproduce.

As such, the churches planted need to necessarily reflect the culture in which they are planted. Their people will have enough work in understanding the depths of sin, grace, and redemption without the added work of learning a new culture. The transmission of the gospel on its own merit will face extreme conditions in any culture, and young

---

1 Merriam-Webster, "Exogenous."

2 Merriam-Webster, "Indigenous."

3 Zannini, "Five Tips for Growing Native Plants."

4 Ibid.

believers within that culture will need assistance — discipleship — in understanding how it is counter to parts of their own particular culture.

The most effective way to plant the gospel in a new culture is to be as free of external cultural influence as possible. Missiologist Ed Stetzer wrote that the task of mission is to transplant the gospel into a new community so that the church could become "native" there.[5]

If thriving, reproducing, native churches are the end goal of our work in mission, then we must protect the indigeneity of the churches among those to whom we are called. It is in those native churches that indigenous people will find the comfort and freedom to explore the gospel and the life-change that comes with it without the cumbersome weight of learning another culture in order to understand it.

## Facades

In April, 2011, I traveled to Lima, Peru, for a series of meetings with missionaries from all over the world. As is my custom, I arrived a day early to explore the city. It was my first visit to this beautiful South American city, and I was excited to experience it and learn about its people.

Having lived in Western Europe for the last ten years, I have grown accustomed to wandering into old church buildings. Europe is filled with cathedrals and chapels looming on street corners, big, beautiful, and mysterious. Many are now museums, art galleries, pubs, night clubs, or even mosques.

While walking around Lima, I came across churches that made me feel as though I was transported back to Spain. The facades of the churches looked very similar, as if they could have been designed by the same architect centuries ago. The interior was very much the same as well, apart from different icons and statues.

In the 15th Century, the Spaniards came into South America bringing with them European colonialism, and the Spanish architecture in those churches reflects just that. It is as though Spain moved into South America, building culture, including church buildings, just like it was back home.

Of course, people and cultures were present in South America before the Spaniards arrived. Just as in other instances of colonization, the cultures of the indigenous people were written off as heathen and

---

5 Stetzer, "Indigenous Church Planting."

Spanish culture was deemed Christian. Spanish church buildings were then built, and Spanish Christian evangelization began, ignoring the cultural nuances of the people they were evangelizing.

Spanish Catholics weren't the only ones to export their religious culture in the name of mission. Similar examples exist in evangelical missions over the last 50 years. The effects of exporting religious culture are obvious—tribal African preachers who feel they must always wear a coat and tie to preach and developing countries whose people live in huts worshiping in church buildings constructed in the form of Southern American architecture. It is not uncommon for churches to simply export their model of church from their current setting into another city and context abroad.

One well-meaning church wanted to help a missionary reach his city by starting a cutting-edge church service. The church's strategy was to literally put all they needed including chairs and sound equipment into a crate and ship it to Europe. They even offered to translate their pastor's videos into the host language each week to be played at the service. They believed all the missionary needed to do was find an attractive venue and turn on the DVD player.

No doubt the intentions of the church were good, but they started with a faulty assumption—if it works here, it must be good anywhere. The natural next step in that process of thought was to export their good and useful product. The problem is that there was no consideration given to cultural context, which is always a huge barrier for the gospel.

## My 2001 Journey to Europe

When moving overseas, either as an international businessperson or a full-time Christian worker, people are faced with deciding what to take with them as they start their new life. Many choose to sell everything and buy all new furniture, clothing, and supplies once they arrive in their new host country. This process can be helpful in immersing them fully and immediately in the new culture, but it can be cost-prohibitive and overwhelming.

Other people choose to crate their belongings and ship them to their new location. This approach brings certain benefits. Big- ticket items are already paid for which can save a great deal in both financial resources and in time spent shopping for new items. In addition, some degree of familiarity remains in a home when its furnishings are a recognizable part of a person's old life.

When my family and I prepared to go overseas in 2001, we began weighing our options. We knew we would be downsizing our living space, but we had no idea how much space we would actually have in each room. We did not know if our king-size bedroom suite would fit in our new place, or if we would have space for the piano that had been handed down to us through my family.

Considering that the United States dollar was in a favorable position against the Euro at the time, we decided to sell all of our furniture and buy new once we arrived in Spain. We were so proud of ourselves for making an intentional decision to be European and start from scratch. We were also really looking forward to raiding the local IKEA store.

Then the reality of our decision set in. We had to reduce all we owned to the thirteen pieces of luggage we were allowed by the airline. We laid it all out on my parent's basement floor and began to narrow it down. The oversight in our plan became glaringly obvious: What would we do with all of our books? In a time before Kindles, iPads, and Nooks, I had no idea how I would transport my library of church-planting books to Europe. These books had revolutionized the way I planted churches in the US. How could I possibly survive without them in my new context?

We found a solution through the US Postal Service, which would send a single box weighing up to 50 pounds for $30. Our tight budget allowed for five boxes at that price. Being a good husband and father, I told my family that they could each have a box, and I would have two. After all, the church-planting movement in Europe was completely dependent on my resources and ability. My family packed their boxes full of Veggie Tales, Star Wars, and Disney books, videos, and memorabilia, and I loaded my church-planting resources and a few commentaries.

I knew it would take around 30 days for our cargo to arrive, so I mailed the boxes in just enough time for them to arrive at the same time we did. My plan was near-perfect. When we arrived in Spain, we found two boxes waiting for us, one filled with my son's belongings and the other with my daughter's. We began settling into our new home, which would not have held our king-size bed, and waited eagerly for the other boxes to arrive. A year later, a box full of women's devotionals showed up at my parents' house back home in the US. It was my wife's box.

At the time of this writing, it has been almost eleven years, and I am still waiting on my two boxes of church-planting books. I've still got my fingers crossed, though. There is yet hope for that church-planting movement in Europe!

I often wondered about God's greater purpose for me not receiving my books. I saw at least a couple of positive results from this mishap. First, I had to concentrate on learning Spanish since all of my English books were gone, which is really what I needed to be focused on anyway. More importantly, since I did not have my church-planting books, I had to rely solely on Scripture and the direction of the Spirit. I realized in the process just how much we relied on programs and methodologies in church planting.

I used my circumstance as an opportunity to start over. I started reading the book of Acts from a new perspective, a new cultural context. I was not able to simply transfer my North American church-planting methods to a different culture. I had to learn the language and cultural nuance in order to understand how the gospel applied and what the church would look like there. The unspoken goal for me changed from planting American-style churches to allowing the gospel to transform lives within a Spanish context. From that soil would spring up a church deeply rooted in the culture, something indigenous — something at home there. It would not require people to be American in order to be Christian.

## Indigenous Churches

British missionary Roland Allan wrote that "an indigenous church, young or old, in the East or in the West, is a church which, rooted in obedience to Christ, spontaneously uses forms of thought and modes of action natural and familiar in its own environment." Missiologist Alan Tippett added his thoughts to the conversation, "When the indigenous people of a community think of the Lord as their own, not a foreign Christ; when they do things as unto the Lord, meeting the cultural needs around them, worshipping in patterns they understand; when their congregations function in participation in a body which is structurally indigenous; then you have an indigenous church."[6]

---

6 Ibid.

As we see in these definitions, indigenous churches are simply rooted in the cultural context from which they arise, and include thought and action common to the culture within their worship practices. Particularly, Tippett's definition speaks to why indigeneity is even important: It helps people understand Christ as their own Lord, not a foreign God. They see Christ not as the God of people completely different than them, but as Who He actually is—the God of all of the diverse peoples of the world.

Therefore, indigenous churches are incredibly important for mission, as well. Indigenous churches live and worship in a manner that the cultures in which they are rooted understand. Cultural barriers that exist between those cultures and an American church, for instance, don't exist with indigenous churches. In short, when indigenous churches are on mission in their own particular culture, they are unhindered by cultural differences and expose the clear difference between people transformed by the gospel and those who are not. The life-changing power of the gospel is unimpeded by cultural barriers.

Being indigenous affects much more than simply the church planter. It is more about the nature of the church as a whole than simply who the church planter is. However, the church planter influences the church much like the horticulturist influences the growth of plants. Consider this North American scenario from Ed Stetzer:

> A church planter [in Chicago] may be from Chicago, but if the church is dependent on offerings from Alabama, has adopted an Alabama style of worship, and meets at the time that the farmers in Bessemer, Alabama set 100 years ago, the church may not be indigenous for Chicago (though perhaps it would be in Bessemer). The origin of the church planter is not the determining factor of being indigenous. Instead, the nature of the church plant is. A person from Chicago is more likely to lead an indigenous church because he has been raised in that area. However, if education or other influences are non-indigenous in nature, the church planter might start a church that is out of place in the local culture.[7]

If we follow this idea to its logical conclusion, an indigenous church is the proof of the gospel being incarnated within a certain

---

7 Ibid.

cultural context. The lack of indigenous expressions and the presence of foreign ones prove a lack of cultural insight and care for the local people. To go to the "all peoples" of the Great Commission, we need to plant the unchanging gospel into new cultural soil and let it take root there.[8]

## How Do We Protect Indigeneity?

Again, Roland Allen challenged the church to champion indigeneity in his book Missionary Methods: St. Paul's or Ours?, he listed five main ways missionaries can protect indigeneity.

- The teachings must be easily understood so that those who listen can retain it, use it, and pass it on.
- Churches and organizations in the new culture should be set up in a way that national Christians can maintain them.
- Church finances should be provided and controlled by the local church members.
- The Christians should be taught to provide pastoral care for each other.
- Missionaries should give national believers the authority to exercise spiritual gifts freely and at once.[9]

As I read these five practical steps toward protecting indigeneity, I see five underlying principles that must be practiced as we develop missionary strategy.

## Understanding Cultural Context

When engaging any cultural context with the gospel, understanding the culture is a priority. When people must abandon their valued cultural identity and adopt an alien culture in order to become believers, the cause of church planting will not go far. Around the world, many churches that appear culturally out of place in their setting serve as testimonies to this obstacle. In too many instances, church planting has become cultural warfare, as missionaries and local Christians attempt to conquer and change the culture rather than the

---

8 Ibid.

9 Allen, *Missionary Methods*, 151.

hearts of the people. Whenever one must become like a Russian, American, European, or any other culture foreign to his own to become a Christian, there is little chance that the movement will spread rapidly among those people.

Luke's account of the Judaizers gives in Acts 15 holds special significance here. "But some men came down from Judea and were teaching the brothers, 'Unless you are circumcised according to the custom of Moses, you cannot be saved' " (Acts15:1). This group of believers loyal to their Jewish traditions was telling Gentiles that they must first be circumcised in order to follow Jesus. In doing so, the group was actually derailing what God was doing among the Gentile converts by adding non-biblical requirements for being a Christ-follower.[10]

## Reproducing Disciples

My early church-planting experience occurred in the US. Looking back over those years, I can see that instead of planting churches, my team and I actually became quite proficient at planting church services. We could attract a crowd with our cool band, appealing video clips that fit nicely with our theme, dramas that set the tone for the message quite nicely, and relevant preaching. We placed a high value on excellence and demonstrated it through quality child care, friendly greeters, good signs, and great coffee.

The majority of our focus was on the Sunday gathering. It became the starting point for every ministry instead of a celebration of what was happening throughout the week. As a result, we focused the majority of our time and resources on making the church gathering experience meaningful and we short-changed discipleship. Simply put, we focused on producing quality church services instead of reproducing disciples. Instead of understanding the culture and needs of the people around us and allowing the gospel to address those needs, we designed services and called everyone to come to us.

Since moving overseas, I have regularly written newsletters to our supporters in the US to communicate prayer requests, needs, and praises. I seldom received many comments on my newsletters until one particular occasion when I wrote about preaching at a church on the mission field. I had been in Spain for about a year, and I had struggled

---

10 More about understanding the cultural context in the chapters, "Contextualization" and "Exegeting Culture."

to learn the language. Finally, after making some progress, I was invited to preach in a local church. After I sent my newsletter out detailing the opportunity I had to preach, responses began to pour in from supporters expressing their excitement that I was finally able to begin my work as a missionary and proclaim the gospel.

I do not think any of these people would say that what I was doing before was less important, but their excitement about my involvement in a Sunday morning service betrayed their real expectations for the work I should be doing. When they learned I had actually preached, there was something tangible to hold onto. Their response to me was evidence of the emphasis we have historically placed on the church service. They had no framework for understanding the process of learning the culture or making disciples outside of the worship service setting.

The corporate gathering for worship is important, good, and right; but something is out of place when your focus on making them great diminishes your efforts in mission within the culture around you. It also tends to produce churches shaped by the cultural preferences of a few rather than the indigenous responses of the people there as they come to know Christ as Lord.

There is another way to plant churches, though; one that takes culture into the equation and results in churches that reflect that truth. Planting the gospel in a culture and allowing the culture to shape the churches as they grow within, not removed from, their culture will result in indigenous churches forming around those disciples. Our tendency toward "extractional" discipleship is a hindrance to the process.[11] A simple formula for planting indigenous churches might look like this:

**planting the gospel in a culture**

+

**making disciples within the same culture**

=

**indigenous churches**

It is possible for missionaries crossing cultures to plant indigenous churches, but it requires a humility often missing from the process. We need to learn to play second fiddle. In days gone by, plays would often

---

11 More on this in the "Engaging Tribes" chapter.

feature a single fiddler on stage to accompany the action of the story. A second fiddler would be off-stage and unseen by the crowd who could play just as well as the one on stage. If the fiddler on stage broke a string, the back-up player would begin to play, and the on-stage player would mimic playing to keep up appearances. The crowd would be completely unaware that the second fiddler was there, and he would receive no recognition for the part he played.[12]

In regards to disciple-making, missionaries would do well to practice playing second fiddle. Several years ago, missiologist David Garrison wrote Church Planting Movements based on research of church multiplication around the world and its underlying principles. In the book, he points out that missionaries should keep a low profile as they seek to initiate and nurture the movement. The missionary church planter should minimize foreignness and encourage indigeneity by mentoring pastors from behind the scenes.[13]

For those brought up in a Western culture that glorifies celebrity, even within our pulpits, it may be a difficult task to rethink and reorganize priorities enough to play second fiddle. Doing so, however, paves the way toward raising up indigenous leaders who will lead to indigenous local expressions of the Church.

### Shaping Leaders

Mission organizations have an acrostic for almost everything. One example that deals with raising up leaders is the acronym MAWL. Although it conjures up an image of a grizzly bear attack, it has a much subtler, kinder use in mission circles. The acronym defines the following approach to raising up leaders:

**Model**—Model for them how it should be done and spend time debriefing them in the process, including what and why you are doing what you do.
**Assist**—Let them do the work and you help them as needed and provide real-time coaching.
**Watch**—Observe them as they lead and provide necessary feedback.

---

12 Answers Corporation, "Where does the term second fiddle come from?"

13 Garrison, *Church Planting Movements*, 17.

**Leave**—Identify another potential leader and repeat the process.[14]

Mission strategist and trainer Curtis Sergeant teaches that MAWL is the rhythm of discipleship that contributes to a Church Planting Movement (CPM). This model assists the missionary in training the new believer in planting CPM-oriented churches, watches to see that they and the churches are reproducing, and then leaves in order to begin the cycle over again. Sergeant relates the MAWL model to teaching a child to ride a bicycle, in that the parent "provides a model by riding the bicycle, provides assistance to the child by holding the bicycle as he learns to ride, then watches while the child rides the bicycle by himself, and finally leaves the child to ride on his own."[15]

Jesus appears to have espoused a similar model in the Gospels. He called the disciples to Himself, taught them, ministered alongside them, sent them out, and finally went away so they could accomplish greater things in His absence than they could with Him present (John 14:12; 16:7–11). The same is true for those who are working to disciple people and see indigenous expressions of the Church rise up as a result. The missionary playing second fiddle and eventually even leaving the theater altogether is the most efficient way to see indigenous leaders trained while maintaining their cultural identity.

Missionary and church-planting trainer David Watson described the final, and likely most difficult step of MAWL:

> If the church planter has done his or her job, then the church has seen the church planter model a mature Christian lifestyle and leadership. The church planter has equipped the church to handle the Word of God, pray, and listen to the Spirit of God, and minister to the people around them. As leaders emerge in the new church, the church planter watches them lead and make their mistakes, helps them recover from mistakes by listening to the Word of God and His Spirit, and mature. And at the right time the church planter leaves, knowing that the church is in good hands, the hands of the Holy Spirit."[16]

---

14 Ibid.

15 Muse, "Model, Assist, Watch, Leave."

16 Watson, "Understanding Transition Points–It's Time To Say Goodbye."

Another term used in church-planting movement strategy conversations is "exit strategy." The essence of this conversation has to do with how a missionary plans to effectively leave in order for the work to sustain itself, reproduce, and thrive. While sometimes this is actually a measurable date set in the future, it often has more to do with what the missionary intentionally does and does not do strategically, as he models his work, assists the new indigenous leader, and provides valuable insight or debriefing with the local leader.

Here again we see the need for humility, and the reality of Jesus' teaching that our purpose is to serve (Mark 10:43–44). For the church on mission, leaving, or being left, is a reality as people are equipped and sent for the sake of the gospel. Rightly trained, they will be prepared to bring gospel transformation into their culture and make other disciples of their Lord.

## Reproducibility

The ability of a church to reproduce itself is extremely important in seeing the gospel move to not-yet-believing people. Living organisms reproduce. Churches are living organisms and should multiply. We want to see churches that plant churches that plant  churches. Mission strategists use a well-known tool to measure the reproducibility of the church called the "Three Self Formula."[17] This formula has been used for over 150 years and was first implemented by Henry Venn and Rufus Anderson, a pair of mission executives who headed the largest mission agencies of their day. It defines a mature/indigenous church as one that is self-governing, self-propagating, and self-supporting—the three selfs.

Missionary Douglas Hayward wrote that one of the attractive features of this formula was its simplicity.

Missionaries could actually count the number of pastors, evangelists, and church leaders who were operating under their own support systems, governing their own churches, and proclaiming the gospel to their own people. While it was easy if the missionary had accomplished his three-fold objective, the three-self formula did not really measure indigeneity. Its primary measurement was independence. Every trait of the three-self

---

17 Reese, "The Surprising Relevance of the Three-Self Formula."

formula could be fully operational, but the church might, nevertheless, still be a foreign organization with an alien message.[18]

I once met a national pastor during my work in Spain who led a "church plant," as he called it, along the coast. Having not heard of a Spanish church plant in that city before, I was intrigued and began to ask more questions. As he gave the background of the church, he explained that it was actually 20 years old. I was shocked that a church of that age would still be considered a plant. So he explained that in his denomination, a local body had to be self-supporting, self-governing, own a building, and have 50 members to be considered a church. Their membership of 47 meant they fell short of the requirements, so they were still considered a plant after 20 years. According to these standards it was nearly impossible for a church to reproduce within that culture.

The church on mission must carefully evaluate the standards placed on its work in order to insure reproducibility. In most cases imported metrics are unrealistic, at best. I once heard a North American church-planting expert tell a group of Western European planters that they needed to raise 150,000 Euros before they launched their public services. While this number may be part of the North American model for planting high-impact churches, it is not as realistic in a culture that does not have the same resource pool as the North American church. Not to mention that planting a large program-driven church in a dedicated building may not be the best assumed model for a Western European context. One danger of this message was local believers heard they would need a lot of money to start a church. Many went away discouraged because they knew they could not raise that amount of financial capital. These types of superimposed standards keep churches from being reproducible.

David Garrison addressed the effects of imposing extra-biblical requirements for being a church:

> When a mission, union or convention attempts to require a congregation to have extra-biblical things such as land, a building, seminary-trained leadership, or paid clergy before granting them full status as a church, a Church Planting Movement is obstructed. Christians may have the best of intentions when they impose preconditions before officially constituting a church—

---

18 Hayward, "Measuring Contextualization in Church and Missions."

preconditions usually aimed at ensuring viability of the church before leaving it to its own devices. However, requirements such as building, property and salaried clergy quickly can become millstones around the neck of the church and make reproducing itself all the more unlikely.[19]

Two critical sticking-points affect reproducibility among North American missionaries. First, there is too high a value placed on excellence. Often the excellence level sought by church leadership requires professionalism only attained by highly-trained and highly-paid staff. As a result, ministry opportunities that don't meet the extra-biblical requirements of excellence are cut, and gifted people without professional training are not equipped and used for the sake of the gospel. This pursuit of excellence is sometimes superimposed on our global mission efforts and the churches we plant, rendering them impaired from the beginning, as the resources to maintain excellence on such a high level are rarely available for those missionary ventures.

The second sticking-point is our overindulgent pragmatism. Excellence and pragmatism are related in that as churches strive for excellence, they are constantly on the lookout for best practices, or other peoples' pragmatic approaches to whatever it is they are trying to accomplish. Too often, the result is a church or leadership that believes their way is the most effective and efficient, and as a result their pragmatic approach is transferred into other contexts with no accommodation for cultural difference. This approach is irresponsible at best and dangerous at worst, and it does not engender reproducibility.

## Avoiding Dependency

Missionaries desire for the church to reproduce by itself, but often partnering churches give to the mission effort in an unhealthy way. Even when the church's intentions are perfectly honorable, the wrong manner of support develops dependency on outside resources and ends any hope of reproducibility of the newly- planted work. Churches must prayerfully navigate the waters of partnership and support, including making decisions on providing resources. Providing these types of things is not always bad, but churches, in their zeal to serve and give, can very easily develop missionary efforts that are totally dependent on

---

19 *Church Planting Movements*, 41.

their support for survival. If the church is dependent upon outside support, then it is not indigenous, because it requires something not found in the local soil. Mutually beneficial partnerships are instead based on deeper connections such as common calling, shared vision and expectations, and mutual learning.

These five principles will help us as we develop the tradecraft of protecting indigeneity. We want to see the gospel advance unhindered by additional requirements from the ones who bring it. Protecting indigeneity will allow the church to grow and thrive planted firmly in its native soil.

# FINAL THOUGHTS

[chapter 11]

BY CALEB CRIDER

## Skilled Laborers

Glassblowing is a sight to see. A couple years ago, my family visited an artisan street fair, and the glass blowers' tent drew a large crowd. Something about the heat of the furnace and the glow of the molten glass was mesmerizing. The glassblowers worked as a team, one worked the long blowing pipe while another shaped the cooling glass. The crowd drew closer to watch the craftsmen in action. The way they moved around the hot shop was like a dance. They made it look easy. As spectators, we could only guess what form the glass would ultimately take. The glassblowers gave no hints as to what they were making. Was it a lamp? A dish? It didn't matter, because we appreciated the beauty of the artists at work. The product seemed beside the point.

Watching the craftsmen at work was a pleasure because they were putting into practice all that they had learned. We were part of the experience, but we were spectators. Sure, we appreciated the work being done before us, but one major thing distinguished us from them: skill.

This is a picture of Christians on mission. Currently, church pews are full of Christians who are fans of missions. They support mission work. They value missionary efforts. But they are merely spectators in the process. But God's people are not commissioned to be spectators; they're called to direct participation in God's mission wherever He leads them.

Our vision is for the church to make disciples who are equipped for mission everywhere. When God's people think and act like missionaries, we identify with our Savior and begin to truly serve as His ambassadors in the contexts in which we find ourselves. Best of all, missionary thinking is what has been missing from discipleship in many churches. Despite what is modeled in churches across the country, being a mature Christ-follower is more than taking responsibility for church programs and activities. For many Christians, learning that they have been saved to a greater purpose of participating in God's global redemptive mission is very good news indeed. The brilliance of God's design to use us, His people, as the means for communicating the gospel into culture is that we have access to people. Our daily lives move us in and out of contact with countless unbelievers.

Imagine a soldier, dressed in uniform, sent to war with all the right equipment but none of the necessary training. He likely wouldn't accomplish his mission. In fact, he'd be lucky to survive. Without the necessary training, can he be called a soldier? It would be irresponsible for his leaders to send him out at all.

It is for the purpose of equipping God's people to be on God's mission that we've written this book. It would be irresponsible for us to call all Christians to mission without also introducing the kinds of skills that would make Christians good missionaries. If missionary skills were a vital part of discipleship for all Christians, every church would have a pool of capable and qualified workers ready to serve at the Lord's request, be it right at home or in a far-off place.

By including a chapter on being **Spirit-led**, we wanted to show clearly that obedience in God's mission requires that we follow His lead step-by-step. This is the example set for us by Peter, Paul, and Christ Himself. We reject the notion that such guidance may be considered "revelation" beyond that of Scripture. Listening to the Holy Spirit is what it means to have a relationship with God. His guidance, in full compliance with what we read in Scripture, gives us direction in our missionary efforts. Our hope is that God's people everywhere would become better at listening and obeying the Spirit as we participate in God's global mission. This will save us from our own strategies and methodologies, and will free us from the desire to copy the models and approaches that seem so successful for others. There is no better way to find our place in mission than the pursuit of the Holy Spirit.

Of all the skills outlined in this book, **mapping** is probably the most underutilized by local churches. Perceived familiarity has led us to assume we know our cities and towns while the landscape has changed all around us. If we are to think and act like missionaries where we are, we must reorient ourselves with the lay of the land by investigating who lives where, and by observing the social, economic, spiritual, and cultural divisions that define our pluralistic society. Our prayer is that this skill would be put into practice by small groups and house churches on the most local level; Christians becoming students of their neighborhoods in order to know the peoples we live among. As the information they glean is added to other information gleaned by others within local churches, complete pictures of the social, economic, spiritual, and cultural climates of cities will emerge so that they will understand how to best incarnate the gospel of Christ to the people around them.

All Christians are on mission, but it takes a bit of practice to be able to observe the behavior of the people around us and discern the bridges and barriers to the gospel. In order for the Church to fully join in God's mission, we must learn to exegete culture as we exegete Scripture. **Cultural exegesis** is the skill that will empower God's people in every corner of society to begin to answer how the universal, unchanging gospel truly is good news for the people we live among. Experienced observation reveals even the most "Christianized" idolatry. It puts God's people in the best position to proclaim the good news in a meaningful way.

It may seem overly simplistic to have included a chapter on **building relationships**, but our experience has been that, in general, Christians just aren't good at relating to people. Typically, Christians are accustomed to either being in a position of authority or deliberately isolating ourselves from the world around us in the name of personal holiness. These two postures have hindered our ability to connect with people on their terms. We believe that conversation skills and social graces should be part of basic discipleship. All Christians, even those who are not "people persons," can learn to interact with others in a graceful and genuine way.

The **persons of peace** concept is not a new one and it's certainly not original to us. But Jesus makes the person of peace central to the sending of His disciples in Luke 10. We're leery of formulaic approaches to "finding" persons of peace, but we have seen this understanding provide missionaries a new perspective on those with whom they interact. We would love to see churches everywhere equipping their members to recognize that God is at work before we arrive on the scene, and that He sets "divine appointments" for us. This helps to elevate every interaction with unbelievers to a meeting of representatives: The minister is a representative of Christ bearing witness to a divinely-prepared representative of a social tribe.

Some may disapprove of our treatment of **social tribalism** as it relates to mission. The prevailing perspective on mission is that the church's task is to evangelize every ethnolinguistic people group. But we're convinced that societies are dynamic and changing, and that our role as missionaries requires us to overcome social barriers to the gospel. Immigration and globalization have brought "the nations" to our own neighborhoods, and urbanization has further fractured our societies into subcultures. According to the Scriptural pattern, the Church should be making disciples of all people in the context of their social groupings. We're not talking about "seeker sensitivity" or "personalized, customized church," we're calling for all Christians everywhere to recognize that they have been sent to whatever groups they live among.

Perhaps the most debated topic in Tradecraft is that of **contextualization**. As we mentioned in the chapter, while no one seriously argues against all efforts to contextualize, practitioners can vary greatly in their opinions on the extent to which we should adjust our approaches toward evangelization in deference to culture. We have no desire to stir up debate; our goal is that churches learn to recognize the importance culture plays in a person's understanding of the gospel message. In order to equip Christians to contextualize well, churches must insure that every disciple knows the universal, unchanging gospel and can communicate it well to the people around them.

Until recently, missions was something done not by the local church, but by professional agencies. Our intent with the chapter on **pursuing alternative paths** was to show that the opportunities for missionary service, both at home and internationally, are endless. They reach beyond the traditionally held understanding of "missionary" work and open the door to all believers to actively engage in mission. Our hope is that opening the eyes of believers in the pews to the opportunities available to them will fuel a newfound desire to do so.

We spent months searching for a better word than "indigenous" for our chapter on **protecting indigeneity**. It's obviously jargon from the missions world. But we couldn't find a better way to explain the need for churches to reflect the soil (i.e., the culture) in which they're planted. We believe that it is imperative for missionaries to understand the culture into which they are planting the gospel so that the people in that culture understand it as good news. It is also imperative that the churches resulting from disciples made within that culture produce local churches that are equally and reflective of the cultural surroundings. It is not that the church is dictated by the culture, but that it lives out and proclaims the gospel in culturally appropriate terms.

### What We Left Out

The missionary skill set is much broader than the nine we've introduced here. You likely noticed the exclusion of things like building partnerships in mission, preaching, developing platforms, and leading small groups. We also left out any exploration of security, funding, accountability, and communication. Perhaps we'll save these for another book. Many of these topics are already dealt with in many other places, and tend to be specific to locations and circumstances. While there are already lots of resources on missions philosophy and strategy, we welcome a renewed focus on skills, the nuts and bolts of living on mission in the day to day. When you're equipped to think and act like a missionary, strategy and philosophy come more easily and appropriately.

There are terrific tools at your disposal. Lots of Bible studies, missions courses, and conference workshops that can help you understand God's global mission. But there's no substitute for experience. Follow Christ in step-by-step obedience on His mission and you will develop missionary skill. God is faithful to give us all that we need to do what He's asked us to do.

Now it's up to you to implement these skills in your mission field. We want to see small groups working on mapping projects together so that they can better understand their neighborhoods. Entire churches reorganizing themselves in order to better reflect the contexts in which they're planted. Christians everywhere engaging their neighbors in thoughtful dialog and building genuine relationships. Our hope is that churches would stop trying to import methodologies that seem to work somewhere else and instead begin to actively explore new, appropriate expressions of church without regard to numbers, size, coolness, or ego. The truth is, no one can tell you how to influence a social tribe or contextualize the gospel. These things are done by faithful believers who have been discipled into the missionary mind– and skill set. There are no shortcuts.

Our hope is that God's people from every tradition would take these skills and use them to develop a more Biblical missiology.

## Our Goal

The realtor who maps the spiritual dimension of his neighborhood. The teacher who treats her access to the teachers' lounge as an all-access pass to joining an exclusive tribe. The job foreman who contextualizes the gospel by modeling the "wise man who builds his house on the rock" for his construction crew. These are the everyday missionaries whom the church is supposed to produce. Our prayer is that churches will move from an "insider" mentality to that of an "outsider." Then, and only then, can the church truly assume the missionary posture and perspective of our Lord Jesus. The thoughtful application of basic missionary skills would radically change how Christians relate to the world. For Christians thinking and acting like missionaries, it becomes much easier to avoid becoming entangled in worldly affairs. Priorities become clear, and it becomes much easier to know what to say "yes" to, and when to say "no." On mission, the Christian comes to understand the purpose of his life and salvation.

All Christians are on mission, but not all of us are good at being missionaries. We need to learn to think as ones who are sent, and it takes practice and experience to become good at what we have been saved to do. We encourage you to learn these skills, put them into practice, and teach them in your churches. As you do, you'll be surprised at the opportunities that open up. You'll have a new sense of clarity and purpose that makes it much, much easier to make the lifestyle adjustments that following Jesus into mission requires.

# BIBLIOGRAPHY

Allen, Catherine B. *The New Lottie Moon Story*. Nashville: Broadman, 1980.

Allen, Roland. *Missionary Methods: St. Paul's or Ours?* Cambridge: Lutterworth, 2006.

Answers Corporation. "Where does the term second fiddle come from?" No pages. Online: http://wiki.answers.com/Q/where_does_the_term_second_fiddle_come_from.

Appleton, Kate, et al. "World's Most-Visited Tourist Attractions." *Travel + Leisure*, October 2011. No pages. Online: http://www.travelandleisure.com/articles/worlds-most-visitedtourist-attractions/7.

Bierlein, J.F. *Parallel Myths*. New York: Ballentine, 1994.

Blackaby, Henry. *Experiencing God: Knowing and Doing the Will of God*, Revised. Nashville: Broadman and Holman, 2008.

Blake, Daniel. "Turkey Christian Missionaries Horrifically Tortured Before Killings." *Christianity Today*, April 16, 2007. No pages. Online: http://www.christiantoday.com/article/turkey.christian.missionaries.horrifically.tortured.before.killings/10523.htm.

Bolles, Richard Nelson. "What Color is Your Parachute?" No pages. Online: http://www.jobhuntersbible.com.

Booker, Christopher. *The Seven Basic Plots: Why We Tell Stories*. London: Continuum, 2005.

Bosch, David J. *Transforming Mission: Paradigm Shifts in Theology of Mission*. New York: Orbis, 1991.

Brunner, Jim. "When it comes to strip clubs, Portland has nothing to hide." *Seattle Times*, November 2, 2006. No pages. Online: http://seattletimes.com/html/localnews/2003336880_portlandclubs02m.html.

Calvin, John. *Institutes of the Christian Religion*. Peabody: Hendrickson, 2007.

Coleman, Robert. *The Master Plan of Evangelism*, Revised Edition. Grand Rapids: Fleming H. Revell, 1993.

Dodd, Patton. "A Better Storyteller: Donald Miller Helps Culturally Conflicted Evangelicals Make Peace With Their Faith." *Christianity Today*, June 2007. No pages. Online: http://www.christianitytoday.com/ct/2007/june/10.28.html.

Erickson, Millard J. *God in Three Persons: A Contemporary Interpretation of the Trinity*. Grand Rapids: Baker, 1995.

Frost, Michael. Exiles: *Living Missionally in a Post-Christian Culture*. Grand Rapids: Baker, 2006.

Garrison, David. *Church Planting Movements*. Richmond: International Mission Board, 1999.

Gilliland, Dean S. *The Word Among Us: Contextualizing Theology for Mission Today*. Dallas: Word, 1989.

Godin, Seth. *Tribes: We Need You To Lead Us*. New York: Portfolio, 2008.

Gowan, Donald E. *The Westminster Theological Wordbook of the Bible*. Westminster: John Knox, 2003.

Grenz, Stanley J. *Created for Community: Connecting Christian Belief with Christian Living*. Grand Rapids: Baker Academic, 1996.

Grudem, Wayne. *Systematic Theology: An Introduction to Biblical Doctrine*. Grand Rapids: Zondervan, 1994.

Hannah-Jones, Nikole. "Human trafficking industry thrives in Portland metro area." *Oregonian Live*, January 9, 2010. No pages. Online: http://www.oregonlive.com/portland/index.ssf/2010/01/human_trafficking_industry_thr.html.

Hayward, Douglas. "Measuring Contextualization in Church and Missions." *International Journal of Frontier Missions* 12:3 (1995).

Henry, Matthew. "Matthew Henry Complete Commentary on the Whole Bible: Luke 10." *Study Light*. No pages. Online: http://www.studylight.org/com/mhc-com/view.cgi?book=luchapter=010.

Hesselgrave, David. *Communicating Christ Cross-Culturally: An Introduction to Missionary Communication*. Grand Rapids: Zondervan, 1991.

Hirsch, Alan, and Lance Ford. *Right Here Right Now: Everyday Mission For Everyday People*. Grand Rapids: Baker, 2011.

International Mission Board. "Glossary." No pages. Online: http://going.imb.org/details.aspStoryID=7489LanguageID=1709.
_____. "Definition Of Church," No pages. Online: http://www.imb.org/main/news/details.asp?LanguageID=1709StoryID=3838.

Joshua Project. "What is the 10/40 Window?" No pages. Online: http://www.joshuaproject.net/10-40-window.php.

Keller, Tim. *Counterfeit Gods: The Empty Promises of Money, Sex, and Power, and the Only Hope That Matters*. New York: Dutton, 2009.

Lai, Patrick. *Tent-making: The Life and Work of Business as Missions*. Colorado Springs: Biblical, 2005.

Larson, Donald. *Guidelines for Barefoot Language Learning: An Approach Through Involvement and Independence.* St. Paul: CMS, 1984.

Lewis, C.S. *Mere Christianity.* San Francisco: Harper, 2001.

Lloyd-Jones, Martyn. *The Sovereign Spirit: Discerning His Gifts.* Wheaton: Harold Shaw, 1986.

Logos Apostolic Church of God and Bible College. "Greek Word Study on ἄγγελος." No pages. Online: www.logosapostolic.org/greek_word_studies/32_aggeloj_angelos_angel.htm.

Lynch, Kevin. *The Image of the City.* Cambridge: The M.I.T. Press, 1960.

Maffesoli, Michel. *The Time of the Tribes: The Decline of Individualism in Mass Society.* Paris: Sage, 1996.

Marzal, Manuel M. *The Indian Face of God in Latin America: Faith and Cultures Series.* Maryknoll: Orbis, 1996.

McKee, Robert. *Story: Substance, Structure, Style, and the Principles of Screenwriting.* New York: Harper Collins, 1997.

Merriam-Webster. "Exogenous." *Merriam-Webster Online Dictionary.* No pages. Online: http://www.merriam-webster.com/dictionary/exogenous.

_____. "Indigenous." *Merriam-Webster Online Dictionary.* No pages. Online: http://www.merriam-webster.com/dictionary/indigenous.

Miller, Donald. *A Million Miles in a Thousand Years: What I Learned While Editing My Life.* Nashville: Thomas Nelson, 2009.

Muse, J. Guy. "Model, Assist, Watch, Leave." *The M Blog,* July 2, 2007. No pages. Online: http://guymuse.blogspot.com/2007/07/model-assist-watch-leave.html.

Myers, Joseph. *The Search to Belong: Rethinking Intimacy, Community, and Small Groups.* Grand Rapids: Youth Specialties, 2003.

Newbigin, Lesslie. *The Gospel in a Pluralist Society.* Grand Rapids: Wm B. Eerdmans, 1989.

_____. *The Open Secret, An Introduction to the Theology of Mission.* Grand Rapids: Wm. B. Eerdmans, 1995.

Olson, Gordon. *What in the World is God Doing? The Essentials of Global Missions.* Cedar Knolls: Global Gospel, 2003.

Piper, John. "How can I discern the specific calling of God on my life?" *Desiring God,* November 14, 2007. No pages. Online: http://www.desiringgod.org/resource-library/ask-pastor-john/how-can-i-discern-the-specific-calling-of-god-on-my-life/print?lang=en.

Reese, Robert. "The Surprising Relevance of the Three-Self Formula," *Mission Frontiers* (July–August 2007) 25.

Skybridge Community. "About Skybridge." No pages. Online: http://www.skybridgecommunity.net/about-skybridge.

Spurgeon, C. H. "A Sermon and a Reminiscence," *The Spurgeon Archive*. No pages. Online: http://www.spurgeon.org/s_and_t/srmn1873.htm.

Stetzer, Ed. "Indigenous Church Planting." *Church Planting Village*. No pages. Online: http://www.churchplantingvillage.net.churchplantingvillagepb.aspx?pageid=8589989695.

Story, Louise. "Anywhere the Eye Can See, It's Likely to See an Ad." *New York Times*, January 7, 2007. No pages. Online: http://www.nytimes.com/2007/01/15/business/media/15everywhere.html.

Taber, Charles R. "Contextualization: Indigenization and/or Transformation." In *The Gospel and Islam: A 1978 Compendium*. Monrovia: MARC, 1979.

The Upstream Collective, *The Upstream Collective Jet Set Vision Trip Guidebook, 2011.*

United Nations Population Fund. "Introduction." *State of World Population 2007*. No pages. Online: http://www.unfpa.org/swp/2007/english/introduction.html.

Vanderstelt, Jeff. "Why Throwing Parties is Missional." *Verge Network*. No pages. Online: http://www.vergenetwork.org/2012/02/10/why-throwing-parties-is-missional-jeff-vanderstelt.

Watson, David. "Understanding Transition Points–It's Time to say Goodbye." *Touch Point: David Watson's Blog*, May 2, 2008. No pages. Online: http://www.davidlwatson.org/2008/05/02/understanding- transitions-%e2%80%93-it%e2%80%99s-time-to-say-goodbye.

Wikimedia Foundation, Inc. "Grand Central Terminal." *Wikipedia*. No pages. Online: http://en.wikipedia.org/wiki/Grand_Central_Terminal.

Winter, Ralph. "The Highest Priority: Cross-Cultural Evangelism." *The Laussane Committee for World Evangelization, 1974.*

————. "Unreached Peoples and Beyond (1974 to Now)." *YouTube*. No pages. Online: http://www.youtube.com/watch?v=S8KBHqjId5k.

Wolf, Thomas A. "Oikos Evangelism: The Biblical Pattern." White paper presented at Golden Gate Baptist Theological Seminary, San Francisco, California, 1999.

_____. "Persons of Peace." No pages. Online: http://www.kncsb.org/resources/PersonsofPeace.pdf.

_____. "The City." Lecture presented at Golden Gate Baptist Theological Seminary, San Francisco, California, 2000.

_____. "The Universal Discipleship Pattern." Global Spectrum: New Delhi, 1992. No pages. Online: http://tinyurl.com/76n62bb.

_____. "Urban Social Change." Lecture presented at Golden Gate Baptist Theological Seminary, San Francisco, California, 1998.

Zannini, Paola. "Five Tips for Growing Native Plants." *Chattanooga Times Free Press*, February 5, 2011. No pages. Online: http://www.timesfreepress.com/news/2011/feb/05/5-tips-for-growing-native-plants.

# ABOUT URBAN LOFT PUBLISHERS

Urban Loft Publishers focuses on ideas, topics, themes, and conversations about all-things urban. The city is the central theme and focus of the materials we publish. Given our world's rapid urbanization and dense globalization comes the need to continue to hammer out a theology of the city, as well as the impetus to adapt and model urban ministry to the changing twenty-first century city. It is our intention to continue to mix together urban ministry, theology, urban planning, architecture, transportation planning, and the social sciences as we push the conversation forward about renewing the city. While we lean heavily in favor of scholarly and academic works, we also explore the fun and lighter side of cities as well. Welcome to the new urban world.

www.theurbanloft.org
Portland, Oregon